Lehigh University
Bethlehem, Pennsylvania

Written by Larry Koestler
Edited by Kevin Nash

*Additional contributions by Omid Gohari,
Christina Koshzow, Chris Mason, Joey Rahimi,
Jon Skindzier, Adam Burns, Luke Skurman, Tim Williams
and Eric Sturman*

ISBN # 1-59658-073-9
ISSN #1551-1052
© Copyright 2005 College Prowler
All Rights Reserved
Printed in the U.S.A.
www.collegeprowler.com

Special thanks to:
Babs Carryer, Andy Hannah, LaunchCyte, Tim O'Brien, Bob Sehlinger, Thomas Emerson, Andrew Skurman, Barbara Skurman, Bert Mann, Dave Lehman, Daniel Fayock, Chris Babyak, The Donald H. Jones Center for Entrepreneurship, Terry Slease, Jerry McGinnis, Bill Ecenberger, Idie McGinty, Kyle Russell, Jacque Zaremba, Larry Winderbaum, Paul Kelly, Roland Allen, Jon Reider, Team Evankovich, Julie Fenstermaker, Lauren Varacalli, Abu Noaman, Jason Putorti, Mark Exler, Daniel Steinmeyer, Jared Cohon, Gabriela Oates, Tri Ad Litho, David Koegler, Glen Meakem.

Lehigh Bounce Back Team: David Zwirm, James Lynch, Erica Rubinstein

College Prowler™
5001 Baum Blvd.
Suite 456
Pittsburgh, PA 15213

Phone: (412) 697-1390, 1(800) 290-2682
Fax: (412) 697-1396, 1(800) 772-4972
E-mail: info@collegeprowler.com
Website: www.collegeprowler.com

College Prowler™ is not sponsored by, affiliated with, or approved by Lehigh University in any way.

College Prowler™ strives faithfully to record its sources. As the reader understands, opinions, impressions, and experiences are necessarily personal and unique. Accordingly, there are, and can be, no guarantees of future satisfaction extended to the reader.

© Copyright 2005 College Prowler. All rights reserved. No part of this work may be reproduced or transmitted in any form or by any means, including but not limited to, photocopy, recording, or any information storage and retrieval systems, without the express written permission of College Prowler™.

Welcome to College Prowler™

During the writing of College Prowler's guidebooks, we felt it was critical that our content was unbiased and unaffiliated with any college or university. We think it's important that our readers get honest information and a realistic impression of the student opinions on any campus — that's why if any aspect of a particular school is terrible, we (unlike a campus brochure) intend to publish it. While we do keep an eye out for the occasional extremist — the cheerleader or the cynic — we take pride in letting the students tell it like it is. We strive to create a book that's as representative as possible of each particular campus. Our books cover both the good and the bad, and whether the survey responses point to recurring trends or a variation in opinion, these sentiments are directly and proportionally expressed through our guides.

College Prowler guidebooks are in the hands of students throughout the entire process of their creation. Because you can't make student-written guides without the students, we have students at each campus who help write, randomly survey their peers, edit, layout, and perform accuracy checks on every book that we publish. From the very beginning, student writers gather the most up-to-date stats, facts, and inside information on their colleges. They fill each section with student quotes and summarize the findings in editorial reviews. In addition, each school receives a collection of letter grades (A through F) that reflect student opinion and help to represent contentment, prominence, or satisfaction for each of our 20 specific categories. Just as in grade school, the higher the mark the more content, more prominent, or more satisfied the students are with the particular category.

Once a book is written, additional students serve as editors and check for accuracy even more extensively. Our bounce-back team — a group of randomly selected students who have no involvement with the project — are asked to read over the material in order to help ensure that the book accurately expresses every aspect of the university and its students. This same process is applied to the 200-plus schools College Prowler currently covers. Each book is the result of endless student contributions, hundreds of pages of research and writing, and countless hours of hard work. All of this has led to the creation of a student information network that stretches across the nation to every school that we cover. It's no easy accomplishment, but it's the reason that our guides are such a great resource.

When reading our books and looking at our grades, keep in mind that every college is different and that the students who make up each school are not uniform — as a result, it is important to assess schools on a case-by-case basis. Because it's impossible to summarize an entire school with a single number or description, each book provides a dialogue, not a decision, that's made up of 20 different topics and hundreds of student quotes. In the end, we hope that this guide will serve as a valuable tool in your college selection process. Enjoy!

OMID GOHARI ◯ CHRISTINA KOSHZOW ◯ CHRIS MASON ◯ JOEY RAHIMI ◯ LUKE SKURMAN ◯
The College Prowler™ Team

LEHIGH UNIVERSITY
Table of Contents

By the Numbers............................ **1**	Drug Scene.............................. **103**
Academics **4**	Campus Strictness **107**
Local Atmosphere **12**	Parking...................................... **111**
Safety and Security.................... **19**	Transportation **116**
Computers.................................. **25**	Weather..................................... **121**
Facilities..................................... **31**	Report Card Summary **125**
Campus Dining.......................... **36**	Overall Experience **126**
Off-Campus Dining **45**	The Inside Scoop..................... **130**
Campus Housing **57**	Finding a Job or Internship **136**
Off-Campus Housing................ **66**	Alumni Information................. **138**
Diversity..................................... **70**	Student Organizations............ **140**
Guys and Girls **75**	The Best & Worst..................... **143**
Athletics..................................... **81**	Visiting Campus....................... **145**
Nightlife..................................... **88**	Words to Know........................ **150**
Greek Life **97**	

Introduction from the Author

Senior year of high school is one of the most exciting times in any teenager's life. You've nearly conquered the toughest academic institution you've faced thus far in your young life; you've presumably got an easy class schedule; you've got a great group of friends and your biggest social concern is who to take to the prom. Oh yeah, and then there's a little thing called college.

Not only are you expected to get into a college, but your parents will want you to get into an academically sound school, and you also have to find a university that you will enjoy spending the next four years of your life at. Sound daunting? It can be, and sometimes your first impressions and gut instinct regarding a certain college can be rash or uninformed. Therein lies the beauty of this guidebook.

Back when I was an impressionable senior participating in a nonstop parade of college tours, I never really had a clear-cut number one college that I wanted to attend. I've heard from many students that they'll often find schools that they fall in love with, but none of the establishments I visited truly took hold of me. That is, until one fateful Sunday afternoon in November of 1998.

My parents and I were returning from a long weekend in the D.C. area, in which I visited about 10 schools. The last thing I wanted to do was go on another campus tour, but my parents talked me into checking out Lehigh, a school I had never heard of, in Bethlehem, Pennsylvania. The weather was lousy, and despite the fact that the tour guide was very pleasant, Lehigh became more of an afterthought.

I wound up applying to Lehigh among six other schools. I made four, although I got rejected from the one I liked most. Of the four acceptances, Lehigh had the best academic reputation, so I was encouraged to take another look at it. On my second tour, I fell in love with Lehigh. It was another fairly cloudy day, but something about the enthusiasm of the tour guide and the whole aura of the campus, combined with the proximity of the school to my home (New York City) and the fact that one of my best friends was attending was enough for me to finally choose Lehigh.

Oddly enough, upon entering Lehigh as a freshman I had no idea that the Greek scene was so enormous and that it would wind up playing such an amazing role in my experience. This book will provide you with the lowdown on Greek life as well as over 20 other important aspects of the entire Lehigh experience.

So as you hold this guidebook in your hands, congratulate yourself on an excellent purchase. After many hours of writing, researching and obtaining feedback from students, I've created the most comprehensive guidebook to Lehigh known to man. I wish I had had a copy when I was in the midst of the college search. I hope you enjoy!

Larry Koestler, Author
Lehigh University

By the Numbers

General Information
Lehigh University
27 Memorial Drive
Bethlehem, PA
18015

Control:
Private

Academic Calendar:
Semester

Religious Affiliation:
None

Founded:
1865

Website:
www.lehigh.edu

Main Phone:
(610) 758-3000

Admissions Phone:
(610) 758-3100

Student Body

Full-Time Undergraduates:
4,609

Total Male Undergraduates:
2,806

Total Female Undergraduates:
1,850

Male to Female Ratio:
60.3% to 39.7%

Admissions

Overall Acceptance Rate:
40%

Total Applicants:
9,087

Total Acceptances:
3,678

Regular Acceptance Rate:
40%

Freshman Enrollment:
1,125

Yield (% of admitted students who actually enroll):
31.71%

Early Decision Available?
Yes

Early Action Available?
No

Total Early Decision Applicants:
281

Total Early Decision Acceptances:
104

Early Decision Deadline:
November 15

Early Decision Notification:
December 15

Regular Decision Deadline:
January 1

Regular Decision Notification:
April 1

Must-Reply-By Date:
May 1

Applicant Placed on Waiting List:
2,264

Applicants Accepted From Waiting List:
1,228

Students Enrolled From Waiting List:
51

Transfer Applications Received:
313

Transfer Applications Accepted:
166

Transfer Students Enrolled:
71

Transfer Applicant Acceptance Rate:
53%

Common Application Accepted?
Yes

Supplemental Forms?
Yes

Admissions Phone:
(610) 758-3100

Admissions E-mail:
admissions@lehigh.edu

Admissions Website:
www.lehigh.edu/admissions

SAT I or ACT Required?
Either

SAT I Range (25th – 75th Percentile):
1220-1380

**SAT I Verbal Range
(25th – 75th Percentile):**
590-670

**SAT I Math Range
(25th – 75th Percentile):**
630-710

**First-Year Students
Submitting SAT Scores:** 98%

SAT II recommended, but not required

**Top 10% of
High School Class:**
59%

Application Fee:
$60

Financial Information

Full-Time Tuition:
$29,340

Room and Board:
$8,230

Books and Supplies for class:
$800

**Average Need-Based
Financial Aid Package:**
$23,533 per year
(including loans, work-study, grants, and other sources)

**Students Who
Applied For Financial Aid:**
56%

Students Who Received Aid:
46%

Financial Aid Forms Deadline:
February 1

Financial Aid Phone:
(610) 758-3181

Financial Aid E-mail:
admissions@lehigh.edu

Financial Aid Website:
www.lehigh.edu/admissions/adfinancialaid.asp

Academics

The Lowdown On...
Academics

Degrees Awarded:
Certificate
Bachelor's
Master's
Doctorate

Most Popular Areas of Study:
11% finance
8% marketing/marketing management
7% mechanical engineering
6% accounting
5% psychology

Undergraduate Schools:
College of Arts and Sciences
College of Business and Economics
P.C. Rossin College of Engineering and Applied Science
College of Education

Full-Time Faculty:
441

Faculty with Terminal Degree:
99%

Student-to-Faculty Ratio:
10:1

Average Course Load:
5

Four Year Graduation Rate %:
53%

Five Year Graduation Rate %:
65%

Six Year Graduation Rate %:
67%

Special Degree Options
Arts-engineering
5-year B.A. or B.S./M.Ed. combined degree program
Civil engineering/environmental science
Electrical engineering/engineering physics

AP Test Score Requirements
Possible credit for scores of 4 or 5

IB Test Score Requirements
Possible credit for scores of 4 or 5

Did You Know?

"Brown Cow" was the nickname of the first Lehigh **Brown and White school bus.**

- Lehigh founder **Asa Packer** ran for president of the United States.

- 1972 saw the last **all-male class** graduate from Lehigh.

Sample Academic Clubs:
Accounting club, Alpha Phi Omega service fraternity, Equestrian Club, Gaming Club, Ski Team, Society of Automotive Engineers, Volleyball Club

Best Places to Study
Fairchild-Martindale Library

Linderman Library

Students Speak Out On...
Academics

> "The teachers are mostly accommodating to your individual needs, but don't expect to learn everything in class; stress is put on home study time. Class can occasionally be interesting unless it is an upper-level business class."

Q "I haven't really taken a lot of diverse classes because I am double majoring and minoring, but I feel there are certain teachers who really love to teach, and those classes are enjoyable. There are a lot of **teachers at Lehigh who teach just to teach**, and I think you can immediately tell who they are, and in my experience, their classes seem to be a lot more boring."

Q "The teachers' abilities and interest in their classes **depends on the type of class** as well as their interest in it. I have found that being in the business school, very few of the teachers there provide interesting and thought provoking classes. However, when the teacher is an outside professional and just teaches for fun, they provide a wonderful classroom environment."

Q "**Most of the teachers are pretty approachable** and easy to talk to - especially in smaller classes. I think most of my classes are pretty interesting, once you get past the distribution requirements."

Q "Whether or not the class is interesting **depends completely on the teacher**."

Q "**Overall the teachers at Lehigh are very educated** and know a lot about their subjects. I have had some trouble finding teachers that make class more interesting. I am in the business school and I'm sure this has a big part to do with why I find my classes uninteresting, but I still think the teachers are not fulfilling their part and keeping the students entertained."

Q "Some teachers try to actually teach while others pass time and merely cover the lesson plan. **Some classes are interesting** but Lehigh could use more leisure and lifestyle courses, such as wine-tasting and cooking courses."

Q "My teachers all have been interested in teaching the material and helping students. I might be one of the fortunate ones, but **I have liked and learned from almost all of my teachers.** I find most of my classes interesting, the core classes are more boring than electives, but still keep my attentiont."

Q "One constant I have found about the teachers at Lehigh is that they all care about their students doing well and are always willing to help. **Most teachers have office hours and many go above and beyond by answering e-mails** and even talking to students on the phone. I am a public relations major and find my classes very interesting. I learn about real world events and am able to apply my knowledge and skills to everyday situations."

Q "I think that **the teachers are interesting if you take the time to know them** but I don't think they make a huge effort to get to know you unless you take the first steps. I found my introductory level classes boring and dull. However, as I began picking my own classes and started to find what really interested me I found very interesting classes that I enjoy attending."

Q "The teachers **are very hit or miss** - some suck and are clearly not interested in what they are doing, and some, especially the ones who worked in their field before teaching, are much better and bring the material to life."

Q "**Lehigh has a lot of great professors** with tons of experience in their respective fields. Their real-life experiences really add to classroom discussions."

Q "As in any school, some of the teachers were extremely interesting, others were very dull. Fortunately the interesting ones were not located in just one field of study, so there was a **good chance that you would have at least a few good teachers a semester.**"

Q "While I'm sure that my experience in the school of Arts & Sciences was different from that of people in the other two schools, in general I believe that the professors at Lehigh took their positions because they are **genuinely fascinated** with their subject area."

Q "**The teachers are really hit or miss.** Some of them are engaging and have a good grasp of their subject; some are flighty and have no business teaching."

Q "As a journalism major, I found most of the teachers to be truly **amazing and energetic people**. They were fun to work with and extremely helpful. I found most of the classes within my major to be extremely interesting and fun."

Q "Classes are what you make of them. If you attend, you'll learn the material. If you don't attend, you'll cram for exams and forget everything. But when you have an inspiring teacher you'll **definitely go to class**. You have to ask the older students for advice on teachers; they definitely know which ones you should choose for classes."

"The first year classes (requirements) are very typical and not particularly challenging, but once I got into my major courses I was thrilled with them. The professors are extremely engaging, and in the journalism and English departments, **they are run very liberally** - the professor usually learns as much from you as you do from him."

"As a freshman, you take most of your pre-requisites. This means **big classes for your first year**. However, you also meet once a week with smaller group of students and a TA. The professors I've had have been good, and my TAs have been great. You get the information from two points of view and this tends to clarify things for most people."

"The teachers are a real hit or miss, as they would be in any school. Most, from my experience, were very willing to help if you were willing to put in the time. Due to certain major and minor combinations, students may have a substantial amount of requirements to fill, which leaves less time for electives. **Lehigh continues to be innovative in creating some new and interesting classes**."

The College Prowler Take On...
Academics

The student body is essentially in agreement when it comes to Lehigh's academics – if the professor makes the class interesting, the student will become that much more fascinated by the subject. Students in the business and engineering schools tend to complain more often about boring classes, while liberal arts students seem more likely to praise their professors. A professor's passion for the subject really makes all the difference. Lehigh's workload isn't impossible, but students are frequently kept busy doing either homework, group projects or studying for tests.

The professors at Lehigh are, for the most part, engaging, knowledgeable and friendly. Every professor has office hours, and most are flexible if a student needs to meet outside the delineated hours. Lehigh has long been pigeonholed as an engineering and business school, but over the past few years the administration has made a excellent progress in establishing the credibility of the college of arts and sciences, with the construction of the Zoellner Arts Center within the last decade as well the much-needed recent renovation of Coppee Hall as the new home of the journalism department. In fact, the excellence of the journalism department may be one of Lehigh's best-kept secrets. Overall, Lehigh has certainly earned its solid academic reputation as well as the students' unofficial motto: "Work hard, party hard."

The College Prowler™ Grade on Academics: B+

A high Academics grade generally indicates that professors are knowledgeable, accessible, and genuinely interested in their students' welfare. Other determining factors include class size, how well professors communicate, and whether or not classes are engaging.

Local Atmosphere

The Lowdown On...
Local Atmosphere

Region:
Northeast

City, State:
Bethlehem, PA

Setting:
Abandoned Steel Mill

Distance from Philadelphia:
1 hour

Distance from New York City:
1.5 hours

Points of Interest:
Dorney Park, Banana Factory, Crayola Factory, The Discovery Center, The Bethlehem Star, Main Street, Historic Bethlehem

Closest Shopping Malls:
Lehigh Valley Mall

Closest Movie Theatres:
Regal (Hoyts) Saucon Valley Cinema 10
3717 Rte. 378
Bethlehem, PA
Phone: (610) 814-2340

Valley Theaters Inc. Boyd Theater
30 West Broad Street
Bethlehem, PA
Phone: (610) 866-1521

Carmike 16
1700 Catasaqua Road
Allentown, PA
Phone: (610) 264-9624

Major Sports Teams:
Lehigh University Mountain Hawks
(college football)

Philadelphia Eagles
(football)

New York Yankees
(baseball)

Philadelphia Phillies
(baseball)

City Websites
http://www.bethlehempaonline.com
http://www.lehighvalleypa.com
http://www.lehighcounty.org

Did You Know

5 Fun Facts about Bethlehem:

1. Bethlehem, known as **Christmas City, U.S.A.,** was given its name on Christmas Eve 1741.
2. The Moravian Book Shop, located in Historic Bethlehem, is the **oldest existing bookseller** in the world, founded in 1745.
3. Bethlehem's Musikfest is considered the **largest music festival in the country,** with over 1,000 musical performers and an annual attendance of over 1 million.
4. Moravians in Bethlehem completed the **first known Waterworks system** providing drinking and wash water in the American colonies (1754).
5. The Philadelphia Eagles have held their **NFL training camp** at Bethlehem's Lehigh University for the past three years.

Famous People from Bethlehem:
Asa Packer

Students Speak Out On...
Local Atmosphere

"I wouldn't walk around town, it's very unsafe. There's a nicer part of Bethlehem, but it's not within walking distance, which makes it very hard to get to."

Q "The town of Bethlehem is very centered around Lehigh and its students. **The other residents are hardly involved in our daily lives** but the businesses and restaurants depend heavily on their Lehigh business. The fact that Gold Plus is now accepted virtually everywhere in town is wonderful."

Q "The **Southside of Bethlehem is pretty run down**, but even in the three years that I have been here, it's gotten better and Lehigh students are going off-campus a lot more. Although everything you need is in Allentown, which is only about 15 minutes away."

Q "There is nothing rewarding about the town surrounding Lehigh. However, that doesn't matter because **the campus life is fantastic.**"

Q "**Bethlehem is relatively boring** and fails to provide the students with extracurricular activities. On top of that the people living in the town generally do not get along with the students. There are two other universities present in the town and they come and hang out at Lehigh occasionally. Things to stay away from are some of the bars and the townies."

Q "The restaurants are surprisingly good if you know where to go. **The town is worse than Jersey**, and there is little interaction with other local colleges. There are attractions to visit within a reasonable distance such as Dorney Park and the Crayola factory. Stay away from the townies unless you're looking to get held-up or are in search of a gangbang."

Q "The town that we live in is very urban. I don't feel comfortable walking off-campus by myself. **There are some nice restaurants on the south side of Bethlehem**, but for the most part, the nicer part of town is over the bridge on the north side."

Q "Bethlehem seems to be more beautiful every year. When I first came to Lehigh I felt that the town was dirty, ugly, and unsafe. However, with the help of President Farrington the south side of Bethlehem has really cleaned up and I feel like I live in a real college town. Moravian college is close by, but the campus is generally deserted. **I would stay away from the train tracks and bus station at night**. There are plenty of places to visit in the surrounding area. If it is nice out you can go to Dorney Park or if you want to do something different, the Crayola Factory is only 20 minutes away."

Q "Stay away from everything....except fast food on **Stefko Boulevard**."

Q "The atmosphere is not very good. **It is a pretty impoverished town**, but that means that the majority of students stay on campus, which makes socializing great."

Q "There's a ton of interesting history, and for a large period of time, **Bethlehem's steel mill was one of America's greatest** assets and I think it goes unappreciated by most of the undergraduates."

Q "The atmosphere in Bethlehem is nothing to brag about. **Without the school there is nothing**, and that makes campus the only place you want or need to be. Lehigh is invariably separated from the other colleges and universities that surround it, so unless you are willing to travel a bit to the surrounding cities, be prepared for many nights with the same people."

Q "**Good thing campus life is so much fun, because Bethlehem sucks**. There is hardly anything to do except drink and hang out with your Lehigh friends. The only 'stuff to visit' is the Tally Ho."

Q "Bethlehem/Allentown is kind of a mixed bag. There are some neat places to go in the area, but a lot of it is kind of run-down, and definitely not somewhere you'd want to be late at night. There are plenty of brochures available (they're laying around the student center mostly) on all of the little trips one can take in the area. As far as other colleges, **both Muhlenberg and Moravian are in the area**, but their students always come here to party and not vice-versa"

Q "The **atmosphere in Lehigh's town is nothing like the atmosphere in Lehigh**. The surrounding Bethlehem area is pretty old, run-down, and relatively quiet. Without a car it is a bit difficult to make it to places such as the mall, the Crayola Factory, or restaurants. Regardless of the surrounding area, the beautiful campus makes the experience very worthwhile. There are other schools relatively close, but interaction with them is few and far between."

The College Prowler Take On...
Local Atmosphere

It's no secret that the town of Bethlehem isn't exactly New York City, but there have been improvements over the last few years to help improve the economy, most notably on the south side, nearby campus. The north side, or historic Bethlehem, is five minutes from campus by car and has always been charming. A stroll down Main Street can make you feel like you're from a completely different era, with the old-fashioned sidewalks and storefronts. Both south and north sides have their share of distinct eateries, and the north side actually has some surprisingly good restaurants. Aside from the food, most students will agree that there's not a whole lot to do in Bethlehem, but the lack of an exciting town is more than made up for in the excellent social life on campus. Students with cars often drive to Allentown for most of their needs.

While most people are somewhat skeptical of Bethlehem upon first visiting, the former steel titan has a way of growing on Lehigh students. The relationship between residents of Bethlehem (townies) and the students is amicable at best; townies don't exactly love the students but at the same time realize that they are the source of the city's money. There's nothing in particular to stay away from other than a few sketchy spots off-campus. Dorney Park and the Crayola Factory are 20-minute drives, Moravian College is right across the river in historic Bethlehem and Muhlenberg College is a 15-minute drive away. The Lehigh Valley Mall and Best Buy in Allentown are also about 15 minutes away and are visited fairly often, although most Lehigh students are having too much fun to be bothered going anywhere.

The College Prowler™ Grade on
Local Atmosphere: C

A high Local Atmosphere grade indicates that the area surrounding campus is safe and scenic. Other factors include nearby attractions, proximity to other schools, and the town's attitude toward students

Safety & Security

The Lowdown On...
Safety & Security

Number of LU Police:
18

LU Police Phone:
(610) 758-4200

Safety Services:
Emergency Phones throughout campus, T.R.A.C.S. (Take A Ride Around Campus) van service, Lehigh University Emergency Medical Services Response Team

Health Services:
Basic medical services, on-site pharmaceuticals, STD screening

Health Center Office Hours:
Weekdays 8:30 a.m. – 5 p.m., Saturday 10 a.m. – 4 p.m., Sunday-closed

Did You Know?

According to Lehigh's rulebook, if a fraternity house has 50 people or more hanging out, it constitutes an unregistered party and **the fraternity can be subject to probation**. Despite this policy, the rule is regularly flaunted by fraternities and the police will often look the other way as long as parties haven't gotten too out of hand. After all, they know where the money comes from, and cracking down on every party isn't exactly the best way to attract students to your school.

Students Speak Out On...
Safety & Security

> "I've always heard of violence on campus but in four years I've never seen anything besides the normal fraternity against fraternity fight."

Q "On campus, the security and safety has become more optimal in past years. The **blue boxes to call the police** and their constant rounds make the campus much more inviting."

Q "I usually feel pretty safe here, especially on the Hill, since there are always police around. However, when I am off-campus, **I never like to be alone.**"

Q "**Police seem to be all over the place**. I would consider the campus safe."

Q "The **security and safety on campus is pretty loose**. People come and go on our campus almost too freely."

Q "**My car got stolen**. That's all I'm saying on that note."

Q "On campus, the **security and safety is above average**. I feel safe walking anywhere on campus by myself during the day or at night. There are always cops and it is a very safe place."

Q "**There is a lot of security on campus**. There are bike cops, brownies and cop cars. There is also the T.R.A.C.S. van service which takes kids on and off the Hill. I would not walk alone at night, but I wouldn't do that anywhere. Also I do feel safer on campus then directly off-campus."

- "Security is fine pretty much on campus; it may actually be too tight. It's horrible three steps off-campus though, where people can **get robbed at gunpoint**."

- "**Safety is the same as at other college** and university campuses. If you put yourself into an unsafe situation, then you could be at risk. You just have to make careful decisions."

- "**It is pretty good on campus,** but off-campus there is definitely some danger."

- "**On campus, very safe**, and the cops may even go a bit overboard. Off-campus is the exact opposite – cops are more worried about breaking up keg parties then keeping the town safe."

- "The **Lehigh police are everywhere** and their biggest responsibility is responding to the age-old crime of college students drinking beer. Lehigh students mostly just have contempt for them."

- "Well, since two of my friends were recently robbed at gunpoint by 14-year-olds, I'm going to go with it's not that great. **I felt safe while I was at Lehigh for the most part**."

- "It's decent; I've never personally had a problem but **knew a few people who were mugged**."

- "The security on campus is very well-refined. The Campus **Police is made up of well-qualified, experienced police officers**, and the chief takes his job very, very seriously. Then there are the 'brownies,' these guys are the campus security. If you go here you will see them around everywhere. They look harmless, but they're also very serious about keeping people safe."

Q "On campus I feel very secure. There are campus cops, which we call Brownies, who drive through the campus during the day and become even more abundant at night. **There are emergency call boxes scattered throughout campus**, each marked with a strong red light. In case of anything, you just run up to one and hit the emergency button and the cops are supposedly there in seconds. I say 'supposedly' because neither I, nor anyone I know, have ever needed the use of one before."

Q "The neighborhood surrounding Lehigh is not one of the best neighborhoods. Just don't walk around all by yourself off campus when it's dark outside. Not a good idea. But don't worry, the guys here are always willing to walk girls home at night. And there's **a van service called T.R.A.C.S. that drives through campus** all night long. If you jump on it, it can take you anywhere you ask. Everyone loves T.R.A.C.S."

Q "On campus, **there are emergency phones all over the place**. If you're walking late at night, they have an escort service that you can call. I've always felt very safe on campus – it's off-campus that you have to worry about."

Q "Security and police are available if necessary. Due to the abundance of Greek life at Lehigh, **campus police are always keeping an eye on things** to keep order around campus. Swipe cards are necessary to get into dorms and sorority houses."

The College Prowler Take On...
Safety & Security

Lehigh students feel incredibly safe on campus, and in certain cases the police can seem almost too overbearing. Off-campus is where the problem lies. The areas immediately surrounding campus aren't terrible; but a few blocks either east or west of campus can be considered somewhat dangerous, especially at night. The Lehigh police force does an excellent job of keeping the campus safe, although at times it seems like the main part of their job entails breaking up parties and busting students for underage drinking rather than doing actual crime-fighting.

Walking around on campus is almost always safe no matter what time of night it is, as there are emergency call boxes situated all over campus. The vehicular entrance to the Hill is even policed on weekend nights to ensure that only Hill residents are driving up to their houses. While this policy can be annoying to non-Hill residents looking to drive up there, it was enacted in response to the increasing amount of townies that used to attend fraternity parties, and as a result has lessened crime on the Hill. Students who live off-campus tend to experience a bit more crime, but as long as people take the right precautions and don't put themselves in unsafe situations, living off-campus should be relatively crime-free.

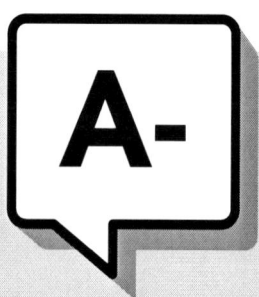

The College Prowler™ Grade on
Safety & Security: A-

A high grade in Safety & Security means that students generally feel safe, campus police are visible, blue-light phones and escort services are readily available, and safety precautions are not overly necessary.

Computers

The Lowdown On...
Computers

High-Speed Network?
Yes.

Wireless Network?
Yes.

Number of Computers:
572

Operating Systems:
PC
Macintosh

Discounted Software
Windows XP available to students that opt to pay the Technology Fee

Free Software:
ACL, Acrobat Reader, ArcExplorer, FTP Explorer, Ghostscript, GSView, Norton Antivirus, PowerPoint viewer, Stunnel

24-Hour Labs
Grace Hall

Charge to Print?
No

Did You Know?
The Department of Journalism and Communication recently moved into newly renovated Coppee Hall, and was provided **40 brand-new Dell desktop flatscreen PCs.**

Students Speak Out On...
Computers

> "Computer labs are accessible 24 hours a day but definitely bring your own computer, labs can get packed and it's annoying to walk up and down those hills in the winter."

Q "**Yes, definitely bring your own computer.** There are a decent amount of computers on campus, but having your own is definitely a plus."

Q "The computer network is extremely helpful. Having your own computer is much more beneficial than always **depending on the computer** labs as they are sometimes crowded and constant internet access is very helpful when most teachers communicate electronically."

Q "I pretty much just use my laptop in my room. I would say basically **everyone brings a computer.**"

Q "Usually you can obtain use of a computer if you need one but it is always better to **have one in your room** as well."

Q "The network is actually pretty efficient and rarely crash. The computer **labs are crowded but you can always find an open computer somewhere** on campus. You just need to know where to look. Incoming students should definitely bring their own computer."

Q "**Definitely bring your own computer.** Unlike some schools I don't really think it is that advantageous to have a laptop versus a desktop, but it doesn't hurt. Yes the computer labs are always crowded and if you have to print something out before class leave yourself at least 20 extra minutes. The network is decent although most of the computers have seen better days. The school provides each student a personal drive in which they can store their work and then access it from any of the computers hooked up to the network."

Q "I brought my own computer with me. The network is very good. I don't know that much about computers, but I know that mine works and if there are any problems the WIRED staff will come to my room and help. **I have never had a problem getting a computer in any of the labs**. I think it safe to say that most everyone here has their own computer."

Q "**The computer network is generally reliable**. If I have any problems I just contact a WIRED person to help me. The computer labs are generally crowded at night, but tolerable during the day. I would definitely bring my own computer and I would highly recommend bringing a laptop."

Q "**Computer network is good and fast**, computer labs are generally crowded except for Grace Hall, which never has any paper."

Q "**It makes life a lot easier if you bring your own computer to school**. It's not impossible to find a computer in one of the labs on campus, but if you have the option of bringing your own, definitely take it."

Q "**Definitely bring your own computer**. It isn't a necessity, but it will make your life much easier, both for school and for socializing."

"**Lehigh provides several computer labs**, but around finals time it really pays to have your own computer."

"**Computing facilities are decent**. There are usually available computers in the labs, but most students bring their own computer."

"**You can bring your own** or use one of the many labs on campus. I never had a problem with finding or using one while I lived on or off campus."

"You can usually find a computer to use in the labs, though during midterms or finals it's a little more difficult. In any case, I would **definitely recommend bringing your own computer** because the freshman dorms are a hike to the computer labs and almost all of your classes requires computer work."

"**The network is great!** It's so fast! There are two big libraries on campus and they both have a ton of computers. I would bring your own though. When you see the amount of work you get bombarded with, it's nice to have the freedom to do it in your own room instead of having to run around every time you need to get something done."

"Personally, I think if every student can bring his/her own computer it is much more convenient. **There are numerous computer labs on campus to choose from**. Labs are not always crowded and if a student had to wait for a computer, he/she would not have to wait very long."

The College Prowler Take On...
Computers

Almost all Lehigh students will agree that the campus computer network is reliable and fast. There are plenty of computer labs which enable most students to get access to a computer whenever they need one. Obviously the computer labs are busiest during midterms and finals, but intrepid students usually can find a computer after a bit of searching. Despite the fact that there are plenty of computers readily available, most students bring computers with them anyway, especially freshman, as it can be a pain to trek down to the libraries, especially during Bethlehem's cold winters. Students who have trouble with their PCs can call the WIRED service, which has normal business hours, and schedule an appointment with a computer technician. The WIRED techs are extremely knowledgeable and helpful.

It's also desirable to have your own computer given the explosive popularity of Instant Messenger. Since the campus is hooked up to a T1 connection, most students are online 24 hours a day, and it has become something of a pastime in and of itself to IM friends rather than taking the extra time to call, especially those of the long distance variety. Checking people's away messages has also become the ultimate procrastination tool. Overall, you'll be happier with your own computer at just about any college than without one.

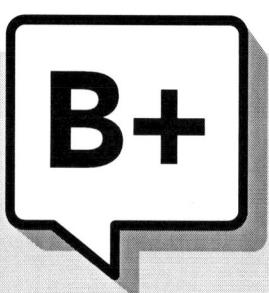

The College Prowler™ Grade on
Computers: B+

A high grade in Computers designates that computer labs are available, the computer network is easily accessible, and the campus' computing technology is up-to-date.

Facilities

The Lowdown On...
Facilities

Libraries:
1

School is a member of library consortia?
Yes.

Campus Size in Acres:
2000 Acres

Museums or special academic buildings on campus:
Zoellner Performing Arts Center; Art Galleries Museum (located in the Performing Arts Center)

What Is There to Do On Campus?
Many students go to the gym between classes, take a jog around Lehigh's steep and hilly campus, or relax on the lawn of the University Center.

Movie Theatre on Campus?
Yes, Kenner Movie Theater, Ulrich Student Center

Bowling on Campus?
No

Bar on Campus?
No, but there are two bars less than a block from the Union.

Coffeehouse on Campus?
Yes. Jazzman's Cafe, Campus Square

Favorite Things to Do:
The Zoellner Arts Center is host to entertainment of all kinds—plays, musical acts, ballet, art exhibits. Although these activities tend to attract older residents of Bethlehem, students are slowly attending more events. There's no real area where students come together and congregate—Lehigh students have a tendency to bond very tightly with the people they live with, so a lot of time is spent in the dorms. Brand new Campus Square has outdoor seating and students are beginning to take to it.

Students Speak Out On...
Facilities

> "The facilities are very nice on campus, although the gym could use a refurbishing and some more equipment. The gym's adequate for a good workout, but could be better."

Q "The facilities are really nice although some of the academic buildings could be nicer. For the most part facilities are really **modern and good**."

Q "**The facilities are nice and constantly being improved**. The computers are all fast and contain almost all programs a student at Lehigh could need. The student center is also very inviting for freshman and upper classmen to meet each other."

Q "Everything is really nice, always **very clean and well kept**. They are always trying to make improvements, and they just added TVs to the gym."

Q "**The facilities are very nice** and are updated and renovated regularly."

Q "The facilities are awesome on campus, except for our gym. The computer labs and student centers **are easily accessible** and provide comfort and security. But the gym at our school totally sucks."

Q "The gym for non-athletes isn't that nice, but **the athletic facilities are BEAUTIFUL**. All of the other student resource centers on campus are very good."

Q "Everything is all nice and fairly new. **The gym is cool but crowded** and the computers are all pretty new. I don't know much about athletic stuff unless the Delta Phi Beirut arena counts, and that is very dirty and beer-soaked."

Q "The facilities are nice, but they aren't quite large enough for the expanding student body**.**"

Q "I thought **most of the facilities on campus were really nice**, except the gym, which I thought could have been cleaner and have more equipment."

Q "Well, if you are on the football or wrestling team, the athletic facilities are pretty good. Otherwise, be prepared to wait through long lines and overcrowded facilities. The **UC is one of the most comfortable places on campus**. Actually all of the buildings are pretty comfortable."

Q "**The student center could use a little work** (threes hardly anything there besides Subversions) but overall the facilities are well maintained and newly renovated."

Q "Everything's nice: **a lot of the buildings have been remodeled recently** and the buildings on campus are gorgeous! Everything is pretty convenient. It's a nice size campus…it takes probably a little under 10 minutes to walk from the bottom of campus to the top. From the bottom to the top is basically one big hill. You have to walk uphill to get to your dorm no matter what, but you get used to it after a while, and it can fight the freshman 15, so there's something positive about it!"

The College Prowler Take On...
Facilities

There aren't many complaints about Lehigh's facilities, save those for the gym. The gym is one of the most crowded facilities on campus, but the students feel it's in serious need of an upgrade. Most of the cardiovascular machines are old and the stationary machines are outdated, not to mention there aren't nearly enough stations. The gym is almost unbearable to be at during peak times (usually right after class ends at 4 p.m.), but those in search of exercise should be able to find solace in the pool, basketball or volleyball courts.

Aside from the gym, Lehigh's other facilities are quite nice; the University Center is a beautiful building and its dining hall is the largest and most popular. The Ulrich Student Center is also pleasant inside, although it could benefit from more shops or diversions. It's also something of a social hub because it's almost impossible not to bump into someone when you go to get your mail. The university bookstore was also recently moved into new accommodations in the state-of-the-art Campus Square dormitory complex, and the new location has helped make the bookstore that much more integral to daily student life. Some complain about the layout of the campus in general, what with it being on a giant hill and all, but many would argue that the peaks and valleys are what give the school its character.

The College Prowler™ Grade on
Facilities: B+

A high Facilities grade indicates that the campus is aesthetically pleasing and well-maintained; facilities are state-of-the-art, and libraries are exceptional. Other determining factors include the quality of both athletic and student centers and an abundance of things to do on campus.

Campus Dining

The Lowdown On...
Campus Dining

Freshman Meal Plan Requirement?
Yes

Meal Plan Average Cost:
$2,036

Places to Grab a Bite with Your Meal Plan

Baker's Junction
Location: 2nd floor of the University Center
Food: Bagels, muffins, coffee
Hours:
Monday - Friday
7:30am - 6:00pm
Saturday & Sunday
11:00am - 4:00pm

Bag-It Convenience Store
Location: Next to Rathbone Dining Hall
Food: Groceries
Hours:
Monday - Thursday
11:00am - 7:30pm
Friday
11:00am - 2:30pm
Saturday & Sunday
Closed

Brodhead House Cafeteria
Location: First floor of Brodhead House
Food: American
Hours:
Breakfast Lunch Dinner
Monday - Thursday
7:30am - 9:30am 11:00am - 1:15pm 5:00pm - 6:30pm
Friday

Brodhead House (Cont...)
7:30am - 9:30am 11:00am - 1:15pm   Closed
Saturday & Sunday   Closed

Burger King
Location: 2nd floor of the University Center
Food: Burgers, fries
Hours:
Monday - Friday
7:30am - 8:00pm
Saturday   Closed
Sunday 12:00pm - 8:00pm

The Common Grounds
Location: Basement of the Rauch Business Center
Food: Chips, donuts, snacks
Hours:
Monday - Thursday
7:30am - 8:30pm
Friday
7:30am - 1:30pm
Saturday & Sunday   Closed

Cort Dining Room
Location: University Center
Food: American
Hours:
Breakfast Lunch Dinner
Monday - Thursday
7:00am - 9:30am 11:00am - 1:15pm 4:45pm - 6:30pm
Friday
7:00am - 9:30am 11:00am - 1:15pm 4:45pm - 7:00pm

The Food Court
Location: 2nd floor of the University Center
Food: Chips, donuts, deli meats
Hours:
Monday - Friday 10:30am

The Food Court (Cont...)
- 8:00pm
Saturday   Closed
Sunday Closed

Mein Bowl
Location: 2nd floor of the University Center
Food: Chinese
Hours:
Monday - Friday
10:30am - 8:00pm
Saturday   Closed
Sunday Closed

Pandinis
Location: 2nd floor of the University Center
Food: Pizza, Italian
Hours:
Monday - Thursday
10:30am - 9:00pm
Friday
10:30am - 9:00pm
Saturday   1:00pm - 9:00pm
Sunday 12:00pm - 9:00pm

Rathbone Dining Hall
Location: Rathbone has an excellent location, overlooking campus
Food: American
Hours:
Breakfast Lunch Dinner
Monday - Thursday
7:30am - 9:30am 11:00am - 1:15pm 5:00pm - 7:30pm
Friday
7:30am - 9:30am 11:00am - 1:15pm, Closed Saturday & Sunday

Salsa Rico
Location: 2nd floor of the University Center
Food: Mexican

Salsa Rico (*Continued...*)
Hours:
Monday - Friday
10:30am - 8:00pm
Saturday Closed
Sunday Closed

Subversions
Location: Ulrich Student Center
Food: Sandwiches
Hours:
Monday - Friday
8:00am - 1:00am
Saturday 1:00pm - 1:00am
Sunday 2:00pm - 11:00pm

24-Hour On-Campus Eating?
No

Student Favorites
Cort Dining Room
Rathbone Dining Hall
The Food Court
Subversions

Did You Know?

On a campus as hilly as Lehigh's, you better believe the students go **sledding on dining hall trays** when it snows. The most popular place is the hill next to Lower Centennial dormitory, by the Rauch Business Center.

On-Campus places to use GoldPlus:

Lehigh University's GoldPlus is a declining balance program that works like a debit card. Simply deposit money into your GoldPlus account. That account is designated especially for you and is encoded on your Lehigh ID card.

Pastaficio
Location: Campus Square
Food: Italian restaurant

Jazzman's Cafe
Location: Campus Square
Food: Coffee shop

The Cup
Location: Campus Square
Food: Ice Cream

Other Options:
There is a privately-owned truck that parks on Packer Avenue called Rocco's Concessions. Rocco's menu is a veritable smorgasbord of food: hot dogs, pizza, egg rolls, mozzarella sticks, fried rice, hot pretzel, hot soups and of course, deep-fried Oreos.

As of the spring of 2003, many off-campus favorites began to accept Lehigh's GoldPlus:

Off Campus Favorites Now Accepting GoldPlus:

Goosey Gander
102 W. 4th Street, Bethlehem
(610) 868-0176
Food: Deli

Deja Brew
101 W. 4th Street
Bethlehem
(610) 865-2739
Food: Deli

Campus Pizza
114 W. 4th Street
Bethlehem
(610) 867-4636
Food: Pizza

Lehigh Pizza
13 W. 3rd Street, Bethlehem
(610) 866-1088
Food: Pizza

New Street Bridgeworks
4 E. 4th Street, Bethlehem
(610) 868-1313
Food: American restaurant

Billy's Downtown Diner
10 E. Broad Street,
Bethlehem
(610) 867-0105
Food: Diner

Tulum
17 W. Morton Street,
Bethlehem
(610) 691-8300
Food: Mexican

Louie's Restaurant
10 W. 4th Street, Bethlehem
(610) 861-0304
Food: Restaurant

Students Speak Out On...
Campus Dining

"The dining halls aren't too bad on campus but a lot of Lehigh off-campus eateries are starting to take Lehigh's GoldPlus, which is a huge benefit to students. I'd recommend Pastaficio or Subversions on campus."

Q "I eat anything, so **I love the food.**"

Q "I don't like the food in the dining halls at all. Although once you join a sorority or fraternity, you have your own kitchen so you have a **lot more variety** in what you can make."

Q "**The food is fine**; nothing too amazing. After freshman year, you rarely will find yourself in a dining hall. Some good spots right off-campus include Goosey Gander, Deja Brew and Johnny's Bagels."

Q "The **food on campus is good - if you are a Somalian**. Otherwise it's pretty gross."

Q "**I like the buffet in the main dining hall** in the University Center. The only decent place in the food court upstairs in the U.C. is Burger King; everything else up there sucks."

Q "Food on campus is good. **The hotspots are Pandini's and Subversions**. Also, GoldPlus is accepted at a lot of restaurants located right off-campus, so many people eat at those places too."

Q "The food is generally good. The food gets boring after a while, but there are plenty of places and a variety of food to choose from. Hot spots include Pandini's, Subversions, the lower UC, **Rathbone and Jazzman's Café**."

Q "The food is good, but **it gets old pretty fast**. I would plan on going off-campus to eat every now and then to spice things up**.**"

Q "**I am hooked on Subversions**. It's a really good quality sandwich shop, and they take GoldPlus, which comes in handy for those of us without real money."

Q "The **food is typical of college food**, but I think Rathbone is actually pretty good."

Q "The food is decent in the dining halls and **the school has opened up some new eating facilities on campus** which are actually quite good, like The Cup, a new ice cream parlor."

Q "**Freshman year I ate at the Cort Dining Room** (Lower UC), all the time and thought it was fantastic, until I had real food again and realized how bad it actually was. Sophomore year I ate at Rathbone religiously because I was on the volleyball team. The salad bar is amazing. The best places for breakfast are Brodhead (the staff there is awesome too) and the omelet bar at the UC. For dinner I'd say go to Rathbone. If I ate lunch on campus it was usually at Baker's Junction or Pandini's. Can you tell I really like food??"

Q "Well now that I've graduated of course **you can use GoldPlus anywhere** and that's a huge plus: free money = free good food! Rathbone is good if you live in Lower Cents. Brunch is great at the UC on the weekends, but it's tough getting up for that."

Q "**The food really isn't bad**. The dining hall has plenty of variety and I could always find something to eat. For freshman without cars, however, the options of places to eat starts to get old pretty fast."

Q "**The dining hall food is decen**t, there's much more variety after the re-opening of the pizza place on-campus. There's enough variety among the dining options. However, all of this will get old eventually - to solve any food boredom, it helps to order out or borrow a car and head out to one of the local restaurants."

The College Prowler Take On...
Campus Dining

No matter what college you attend, there's not going to be a ton of variation among dining halls. Students will inevitably have a veritable smorgasbord of choices, so even the pickiest eaters should always find something to eat. Most students agree that both the University Center and Rathbone dining halls effectively get the job done, but as you move past freshman year you will seldom eat at on-campus facilities. Those students who join fraternity and sororities will have a cook. In fraternities the cook makes lunch and dinner every weekday and sorority chefs usually just cook dinner. The kitchens are usually fully stocked enough to make just about anything anyone could imagine. Especially when you're drunk and it's really late at night.

There is also a food court above the UC dining hall which houses two atrocious eateries, one Chinese and the other Mexican. There's also a Burger King, a deli, Baker's Junction and Pandini's. There is a sandwich shop called Subversions in the Ulrich Student Center, which is very good. The University also very recently opened up an ice cream shop called The Cup, which students enjoy as well as an Italian restaurant called Pastaficio, which has been received with a fairly tepid response. There's enough variety on campus that if a student so desired, they would probably have enough choices to eat exclusively on campus all four years. But most people wouldn't do that. The food's decent, but the off-campus eateries are where Bethlehem really shines.

The College Prowler™ Grade on
Campus Dining: B

Our grade on Campus Dining addresses the quality of both school-owned dining halls and independent on-campus restaurants as well as the price, availability, and variety of food.

Off-Campus Dining

The Lowdown On...
Off-Campus Dining

Restaurant Prowler: Popular Places to Eat!

Akita
Food: Japanese steakhouse
Address: 2730 Walbert Avenue, Allentown
Phone: (610) 432-5800
Cool Features: The chefs cook right in front of you!
Price: $30 and under per person
Hours: Monday-Sunday 1 p.m. – 10 p.m.

Anna Mia
Food: Italian
Address: 114 W. 4th Street, South Side Bethlehem
Phone: (610) 867-4636
Price: $20 and under per person
Hours: Monday-Saturday Noon-10 p.m., Sunday 1-9 p.m.

Apollo Bar & Grill
Food: Upscale American
Address: 85 W. Broad Street, Historic Bethlehem
Phone: (610) 865-9600
Price: $40 and under per person
Hours: Lunch: Tuesday-Saturday 11 a.m.-2 a.m.

Applebee's
Food: American
Address: 2109 Motel Drive, Bethlehem
Phone: (610) 867-7332
Price: $15 and under per person
Hours: Sunday-Thursday 11 a.m.-Midnight, Friday-Saturday 11 a.m.-1 a.m.

Bay Leaf
Food: American
Address: 935 Hamilton Street, Allentown
Phone: (610) 433-4211
Price: $30 and under per person
Hours: Monday-Sunday 11 a.m.-10 p.m.

Bethlehem Brew Works
Food: American
Address: 569 Main Street, Historic Bethlehem
Phone: (610) 882-1300
Cool Features: Six beers are brewed right in the restaurant
Price: $15 and under per person
Hours: Sunday-Wednesday 11 a.m.-11 p.m., Thursday-Saturday 11 a.m.-Midnight

Blue
Food: American
Address: 4431 Easton Avenue, Bethlehem
Phone: (610) 691-8400
Price: $50 and under per person
Hours: Tuesday-Saturday 1-11 p.m., Sunday 2-9 p.m.

Blue Anchor
Food: Breakfast
Address: 9 E. 4th Street, South Side Bethlehem
Phone: (610) 868-0366
Price: $5 and under per person
Hours: Monday-Sunday 8 a.m.-4 p.m.

Casa Mia
Food: Pizza, Italian
Address: 3711 Route 378, Bethlehem
Phone: (610) 867-6421
Price: $10 and under per person
Hours: Monday-Saturday 11 a.m.-10 p.m., Sunday 1 – 10 p.m.

Colonnade Steakhouse – Radisson Hotel Bethlehem
Food: Steakhouse
Address: 437 Main Street, Historic Bethlehem
Phone: (610) 625-2226
Price: $30 and under per person
Hours: Monday-Saturday Noon-11 p.m., Sunday 1-10 p.m.

Confetti Café
Food: American/Vegetarian
Address: 462 Main Street, Historic Bethlehem
Phone: (610) 861-7484
Price: $15 and under per person
Hours: Monday-Sunday 11 a.m.-9 p.m.

Copperhead Grille
Food: American
Address: 5737 Route 378, Bethlehem
Phone: (610) 282-4600
Cool Features: Copperhead Grille has dancing on Thursday nights
Price: $15 and under per person
Hours: Monday-Sunday Noon – 2 a.m.

Country Butcher
Food: Italian deli
Address: 1850 Friedensville Road, Bethlehem
Phone: (610) 838-1260
Price: $10 and under per person
Hours: Tuesday-Sunday 10 a.m.-7:30 p.m.

Dancing Fish
Food: Japanese
Address: 24 E. 3rd Street, South Side Bethlehem
Phone: (610) 997-0630
Price: $20 and under per person
Hours: Monday-Sunday Noon-10 p.m.

Eastern Chinese Restaurant

Food: Chinese

Address: Bethlehem Square Shopping Center, Route 191, Nazareth Pike

Phone: (610) 868-0299

Price: $15 and under per person

Hours: Monday-Saturday 11 a.m.-11 p.m., Sunday Noon-10 p.m.

The Edge

Food: French/Asian

Address: 74 W. Broad Street, South Side Bethlehem

Phone: (610) 814-0100

Cool Features: Cool Urgan Setting

Price: $50 and under per person

Hours: Lunch: Monday-Friday Noon-3 p.m., Dinner: Mon-Tuesday 5-10 p.m., Wednesday-Saturday 5-11 p.m.

Federal Grill

Food: Steakhouse

Address: 536 Hamilton Street, Allentown

Phone: (610) 776-7600

Price: $40 and under

Hours: Lunch: Mon.-Fri. 11 a.m. – 4 p.m., Dinner: Mon.-Thurs.-Sat. 5 – 11 p.m.

Gregory's

Food: Steakhouse

Address: 2201 Schoenersville Road, Allentown

Phone: (610) 264-9301

Cool Features: Gregory's has tons of early 20th century memorabilia decorating the walls

Price: $20 and under per person

Hours: 7 days a week, 11 a.m.-Midnight

The Grotto

Food: Italian

Address: 4th and Adams Street, South Side Bethlehem

Phone: (610) 867-1741

Price: $20 and under per person

Hours: Tuesday-Saturday 1-11 p.m., Sunday 1-10 p.m.

Gus's Crossroads Inn

Food: Greek

Address: 3760 Old Philadelphia Pike, Bethlehem

Phone: (610) 867-8821

Price: $15 and under per person

Hours: Tuesday-Saturday 1 p.m.-Midnight, Sunday 1-11 p.m.

Hack's
Food: Breakfast
Address: 59 E. Broad Street, Historic Bethlehem
Phone: (610) 868-9997
Price: $10 and under per person
Hours: Monday-Sunday 7 a.m.- 4 p.m.

Johnny's Bagels
Food: Bagels and breakfast
Address: 427 Main Street, Historic Bethlehem
Phone: (610) 861-8229
Price: $10 and under per person
Hours: Monday-Sunday 8 a.m. – 3:30 p.m.

J.P. McGrady's Pub
Food: American
Address:117 E. 3rd Street, South Side Bethlehem
Phone: (610) 868-8925
Cool Features: McGrady's has karaoke on Wednesday nights
Price: $15 and under per person
Hours: Monday-Sunday 11 a.m.-2 a.m.

Main Street Depot
Phone: (610) 868-7123
Price: $25 and under per person
Hours: Tuesday-Saturday Noon-11 p.m., Sunday 1-10 p.m.

Manor House Inn
Food: French
Address: 4508 Old Bethlehem Pike, Center Valley
Phone: (610) 865-8166
Price: $50 and under per person
Hours: Tuesday-Saturday 1-11 p.m., Sunday 1-10 p.m.

Minsi Trail Inn
Food: Elegant American
Address: 626 Stefko Blvd., Bethlehem
Phone: (610) 691-5613
Price: $30 and under per person
Hours: Tuesday-Friday 11 a.m. – 10 p.m., Saturday-Sunday 4 p.m. – 10 p.m.

Musashi
Food: Japanese
Address: 1146 MacArthur Road, Whitehall
Phone: (610) 820-9138

Musashi (*Continued...*)

Price: $25 and under per person

Hours: Lunch: Monday-Friday 11:30 a.m.-3 p.m., Saturday-Sunday Noon - 4 p.m., Dinner: Monday-Thursday 4:30-10 p.m., Friday 4:30 -11 p.m., Saturday-Sunday 4 -10 p.m.

No. 1 Chinese

Food: Chinese take-out

Address: 3703 Route 378, Bethlehem

Phone: (610) 868-2389

Price: $10 and under per person

Hours: Monday-Saturday Noon-10 p.m., Sun. 1-9 p.m.

Olive Branch

Food: Middle Eastern

Address: 355 Broadway, Bethlehem

Phone: (610) 814-0355

Price: $20 and under per person

Hours: Monday-Saturday 1-10 p.m., Sunday 2-9 p.m.

Our Beer Belly's

Food: American

Address: 25 E. East Elizabeth

Phone: (610) 861-8120

Our Beer Belly's (*Cont...*)

Price: $10 and under

Hours: Mon.-Sun, 11 a.m.-2 a.m.

Outback Steakhouse

Food: Steakhouse

Address: 3100 W. Tilghman Street, Allentown

Phone: (610) 437-7117

Price: $25 and under per person

Hours: Sunday-Thursday 11 a.m.-11 p.m., Friday-Saturday 11 a.m. – 1 a.m.

Pane e Vino

Food: Italian

Address: 1267 Schoenersville Road, Bethlehem

Phone: (610) 691-7126

Price: $20 and under per person

Hours: Monday-Sunday 1-10 p.m.

Pasta Bella

Food: Italian

Address: Lehigh Valley Mall, 101 MacArthur Road, Whitehall

Phone: (610) 264-7571

Price: $15 and under

Hours: Monday-Sunday Noon-11 p.m.

Pistachio
Food: American
Address: 341 S. Cedar Crest Blvd., Allentown
Phone: (610) 435-7007
Cool Features: On certain weekend nights, Pistachio could be mistaken for a cabaret rather than a restaurant
Price: $20 and under per person
Hours: Monday-Friday 11 a.m.-11 p.m., Saturday 1-11 p.m., Sunday 1-9 p.m.

Starfish Brasserie
Food: Seafood
Address: 51 W. Broad Street, Historic Bethlehem
Phone: (610) 332-8888
Price: $50 and under per person
Hours: Lunch: Monday-Friday 11:30-2:30, Dinner: Mon-Thursday 5-9:30 p.m., Friday-Saturday 5-10 p.m.

Starter's Pub
Food: American
Address: 3731 Route 378, Bethlehem
Phone: (610) 997-5454
Cool Features: Starters has the most TVs of any bar in the area

Starter's Pub (Continued...)
Price: $15 and under per person
Hours: 7 days a week, 11:30 a.m. – 2 a.m.

Tally Ho Tavern
Food: American
Address: 205 W. 4th Street, South Side Bethlehem
Phone: (610) 865-2591
Cool Features: The Ho has either a DJ or musical acts on the weekends
Price: $15 and under per person
Hours: Monday-Sunday 11 a.m.-2 a.

Best Pizza:
Casa Mia

Best Chinese:
Eastern Chinese Restaurant

Best Breakfast:
Blue Anchor

Best Wings:
New Street Bridgeworks

Best Healthy:
Deja Brew

Best Place to Take Your Parents:
Apollo Bar & Grill

Best Deli:
Country Butcher

Best Bagel:
Johnny's Bagels

Closest Grocery Store
Super Fresh
3691 Route 378
Bethlehem
(610) 691-5011

Wegmans
5000 Wegmans Drive
Bethlehem
(610) 317-1300

Wawa
Fourth and New Streets
Bethlehem
(610) 867-3644

Late-Night Snacking
McDonald's

24-Hour Eating
Wawa

Student Favorites
Brew Works
Apollo
Musashi
The Ho
Gregory's
The Edge
Country Butcher
Hack's
Johnny's Bagels

Fast Food within walking distance of campus
McDonald's
Wendy's
Dominoes
Taco Bell
Subway

Students Speak Out On...
Off-Campus Dining

"Restaurants are great off-campus. We have good delis in Goosey Gander and Deja Brew, fast food at Wendy's, and others. Good higher class restaurants to bring a date to include The Edge, Apollo, Minsi Trail Inn, Brew Works, and Musashi."

Q "There are many different places to eat off-campus, and a lot of them accept gold plus now - **Goosey Gander, Tulum, Deja brew, Casa Mia and Musashi.**"

Q "The **restaurants are all wonderful now due to GoldPlus.** It makes life as an upperclassman much easier and cheaper!"

Q "**There are some good, casual places** off campus and we can use our Lehigh GoldPlus at most of them. Goosy Gander, Deja Brew, Casa Mia, Brew Works are my favorites."

Q "The restaurants off campus are really good. We have plenty of choices in the Bethlehem area, including Starfish, **Ana Mia's and Minsi Trail Inn.**"

Q "**Restaurants off-campus are good.** Very diner-like. The good restaurants are on the other side of the bridge and are a little more expensive than the restaurants on south side, but over all there are a lot of good places."

Q "They are overall pretty good. They have a variety of restaurants to choose from including: Sushi, pizza, Italian, American, etc. I would recommend Dancing Fish and Musashi for sushi; Anna Mia's, **Lehigh Pizza and Casa Mia** for Italian; Brew Works, The Federal Grille, Apollo and the Edge for American; and Goosey Gander and Deja Brew for Deli food."

Q "The restaurants are surprisingly good and there are restaurants in Allentown that are great. Apollo, Starfish and Manor House Inn are all nice restaurants. In Allentown, Bay Leaf, Pistachios and Federal Grill are delicious. On campus, **Deja Brew and the Goose are good** and over the bridge Billy's and Hack's are good for breakfast."

Q "There are some good restaurants. Johnny's is great for hang-over breakfasts. **Blue and Apollo** are both very nice."

Q "**Brew Works and Ana Mia's** are good for freshman because they are both within walking distance."

Q "Deja and Goosey are the only two worth mentioning in my opinion. **Gotta love Deja**, a great place to bring a girl that you actually respect."

Q "There are a lot of nice restaurants off campus, my favorites were **Starfish, Federal Grill**, and of course Brew Works."

Q "The farther you get from Bethlehem, the better the restaurants get. **Some of the best places include Apollo Grill and Blue**."

Q "There are some worthy places in the area. Brew Works is the first to come to mind, as it has an excellent beer selection and pretty good food. **DO NOT go to Bridgeworks,** although it's close to campus, because it's highly overrated and repulsive. Pane e Vino has great Italian food. For fine dining I'd pick the Edge over Apollo Grill any day. The atmosphere may be overrated, but the food is to die for. Try the mushroom soup, it's delicious."

Q "Wegman's is the best place on Earth! Billy's Diner is delicious and they have the best eggs and bacon! The owner is super nice. **Akita has good hibachi-cooked food** and sushi, and definitely beats Musashi. Olive Branch has excellent middle-eastern food and the owner is so nice!! Country Butcher is a great Italian deli on mountaintop!"

Q "Goosey Gander has great sandwiches at really cheap prices; **Deja Brew** is another good option for the same kind of food. The Tally Ho has typical pub food (great wings!) and a great outdoor seating area."

Q "There are some definite hot spots. For lunch students tend to eat at **Goosey Gander and Deja Brew**. For dinner, some great places are Apollo Grill, Musashi, The Edge, Brewworks and Blue."

The College Prowler Take On...
Off-Campus Dining

Despite the fact that most students consider Bethlehem nothing more than a ghetto, the town actually has some surprisingly good restaurants. On the South Side alone there are at least 10 quality establishments, and once you cross over the bridge into historic Bethlehem, you'll find a cluster of very classy restaurants with excellent food. Those students with access to cars will open themselves up to a whole new world of possibilities, as there are some very good eateries in nearby Allentown. There definitely seems to be enough variety for everyone to find a place they enjoy. The biggest surprise to most students upon coming to Lehigh is how many good restaurants there actually are.

On any given day of the week, you'll find Goosey Gander and Deja Brew packed with students clamoring for their terrific sandwiches. For those in need of great food at New York City prices, there's the Apollo Grill, Hotel Bethlehem and Edge restaurants. For good American food at more reasonable prices there are the Bridgeworks and Brewworks restaurants. For students willing to travel a bit farther towards Allentown, there is a terrific sushi eatery called Musashi and a great Japanese steakhouse called Akita. Even the bars in Bethlehem have very good food; the Tally Ho and J.P. McGrady's are both student favorites.

The College Prowler™ Grade on
Off-Campus Dining: B+

A high off-campus dining grade implies that off-campus restaurants are affordable, accessible, and worth visiting. Other factors include the variety of cuisine and the availability of alternative options (vegetarian, vegan, Kosher, etc.).

Campus Housing

The Lowdown On...
Campus Housing

Room Types:

Residence Rooms include standard, prime, and suite-style units.

Standard--students share a large, central bathroom facility (most first-year students are assigned to these rooms);

Prime--students share a private or semi-private bathroom with no more than five students;

Suite-style--students share a semi-private bathroom and a common living area.

Apartments are located on-campus. These units can be two, three or four-bedroom apartments and have kitchens.

Houses are all off-campus and include bedrooms, a kitchen, dining rooms, living rooms, private bathrooms, and laundry facilities.

Best Dorms:

Campus Square, McClintic-Marshall (M & M), Dravo

Worst Dorms:

Taylor College, Drinker

Large Dormitory Residences

Dormitories (freshman): McClintic-Marshall (M& M)
Floors: 3
Total Occupancy: 276
Bathrooms: 12, shared by floor
Co-Ed: Yes, by wing
Percentage of Men/Women: 50/50
Percentage of First-Year Students: 100%

Room Types: Every room is a double and has built-in furniture which includes a desk with bookshelf and light, desk chair, bed, individual closet, drawers, medicine chest with mirror, and storage cabinets for each resident.

Special Features: Each floor has its own TV or study lounge, and there is a large study lounge, kitchen, laundry room, and vending machines on the ground floor.

Centennial II (Lower Cents)
Floors: Six buildings (Palmer, Stevens, Carothers, Beardslee, Williams, and Stoughton) with 3 floors each
Total Occupancy: 262
Bathrooms: 24, shared by floor
Co-Ed: Yes
Percentage of Men/Women: 52/48
Percentage of First-Year Students: 100%

Centennial II (*Continued...*)
Room Types: Most rooms are double occupancy, but there are triples on the first floor of each building. Each room has a bed, desk, desk chair, bookshelf, chest of drawers, medicine chest with mirror, and individual closet.

Special Features: The first floor of each building has a common area with lounge, some having a TV room, game room, study area, and kitchen. Laundry facilities and vending machines are located in the basement of Stoughton.

Dravo House
Floors: 5
Total Occupancy: 270
Bathrooms: 20, shared by floor
Co-Ed: Yes, by wing
Percentage of Men/Women: 52/48
Percentage of First-Year Students: 100%

Room Types: Most rooms are double occupancy, but there are several singles and some triples. Each room provides a moveable bed, desk, desk chair, and dresser and has a closet or moveable wardrobe.

Special Features: There are several small TV and study lounges and one large fully furnished programming lounge with TV, kitchen, and study facilities. There are vending and laundry facilities on the first floor of Dravo, and there is a game room on the ground level.

Drinker House

Floors: 4

Total Occupancy: 134

Bathrooms: 12, shared by floor

Co-Ed: Yes, by section

Percentage of Men/Women: 65/35

Percentage of First-Year Students: 70%

Room Types: Most rooms are double occupancy, but there are several singles and some triples. Each room has moveable furniture with a bed, desk, desk chair, dresser and closet

Special Features: Residents can also make use of the TV lounge, study lounge, kitchen, vending machines

Richards House

Floors: 4

Total Occupancy: 191

Bathrooms: 16, shared by floor

Co-Ed: Yes, by section

Percentage of Men/Women: 60/40

Percentage of First-Year Students: 80%

Room Types: Most rooms are double occupancy, but there are several singles and some triples. Each room has moveable furniture, including a bed, desk, desk chair, nightstand, and a closet

Special Features: Richards has a TV lounge, study lounge, game room, kitchen, laundry facilities, and vending machines on the first floor.

Taylor Residential College

Floors: 3

Total Occupancy: 145

Bathrooms: 12, shared by floor

Co-Ed: Yes, by section

Percentage of Men/Women: 65/35

Percentage of First-Year Students: 33%

Room Types: Most rooms are double occupancy, but there are several upperclass singles. All of the rooms contain moveable furniture including a bed, desk, desk chair, dresser, and wardrobe for each resident.

Special Features: The building is divided into three sections. Each section has a large multi-function room with a kitchen and TV (also known as the Red, Blue, and Center Lounges), and its own study facilities. Taylor residents are selected through an additional application process and it is the only dormitory on-campus to offer substance-free housing.

Dormitories (upper-class):
Brodhead House

Floors: 6

Total Occupancy: 194

Bathrooms: In room

Co-Ed: Yes

Percentage of Men/Women: 54/46

Percentage of First-Year Students: 0%

Room Types: Each suite has two double bedrooms or

Brodhead House (Cont'd...)

one double and two single bedrooms, and all suites have a furnished common area and a private bathroom. The bedroom furniture is moveable and includes a bed, desk, desk chair and closet with drawers for each occupant. The common area has a dining table with four chairs, two lounge chairs, and an end table with lamp.

Special Features: Brodhead has its own dining facility, as well as vending machines, a large TV/game room, and laundry facilities. Each of the upper floors has a kitchenette and a study room.

Campus Square

Floors: 4

Total Occupancy: 250

Bathrooms: In room

Co-Ed: Yes

Percentage of Men/Women: 60/40

Percentage of First-Year Students: 0%

Room Types: Air conditioned two-, three-, and four-bedroom apartments, complete with full kitchen, private bathroom, and fully furnished living room/dining room areas.

Special Features: Campus Square is the university's newest dormitory and houses the University Bookstore, a parking garage, and a pedestrian plaza. In addition, three restaurants are featured at Campus Square: The Cup, Jazzman's and Pastaficio.

Sayre Park

Floors: 4

Total Occupancy: 146

Bathrooms: In room

Co-Ed: Yes

Percentage of Men/Women: 50/50

Percentage of First-Year Students: 0%

Room Types: Most apartments are four-person, while a few house three. All bedrooms are singles and each apartment offers a full kitchen, private bathroom and furnished living room/dining area. All apartments are air-conditioned.

Special Features: Each of the three residential buildings has a common lounge as well as laundry facilities. The commons building is a place for informal gatherings or special events. This building has a fireplace, lounge with a pool table and T.V., kitchen area, tutorial/academic space, and a staff office.

Trembley Park

Floors: 2

Total Occupancy: 176

Bathrooms: One in each apartment

Co-Ed: Yes

Percentage of Men/Women: 52/48

Percentage of First-Year Students: 0%

Room Types: Apartments have one double and two single bedrooms, plus a kitchen, furnished living room/dining room and a private bathroom

Trembley Park (Continued...)

Special Features: The kitchen includes major appliances such as a refrigerator/freezer, an oven and a range. There is a kitchen table with four chairs in the dining area, and the living room has a sofa, lounge chair and an end table with lamp. The complex has its own laundry, vending facilities, and a common area with a pool table and T.V.

Warren Square

Floors: 2

Bathrooms: In room

Co-Ed: Yes

Percentage of Men/Women: 50/50

Percentage of First-Year Students: 0%

Room Types: There are six special interest houses located in the Warren Square Complex. Each house contains single, double, and some triple bedrooms. The rooms have moveable furniture including a bed, desk, desk chair, dresser, and wardrobe or closet for each student.

Special Features: All houses include multi-purpose lounges and study rooms. There is a kitchen and laundry facility in each house.

Number of Dormitories:
11

Undergrads on Campus:
70%

Number of University-Owned Apartments:
3

Bed Type:
Extra-long twin

Available for Rent:
Micro-fridges

Cleaning Service?
Yes, daily

You Get:
Bed, desk & chair, bookshelf, closet or wardrobe, blinds, cable TV jack, high-speed Ethernet Internet connection, free campus and local phone calls.

Also Available:
All residential buildings on campus are now smoke-free

Students Speak Out On...
Campus Housing

> "Dorms are all pretty similar but the most social dorm always seems to be M & M. Stay away from Lower Cents, it has a long walk to night life."

Q "Since they changed the dorm selection policy this year, there aren't really any 'cool' dorms, which is a lot better for the freshman to meet each other. All the dorms I've been in are nice, **definitely not disgusting or old**."

Q "**The dorms are small but also very inviting to freshman**. Living in an all-freshman dorm is much better as it allows you to meet only freshman who are in the same position as you."

Q "The dorms are ok. I would say that **the dorms in the quad (Drinker, Dravo and Richards) are the best options**. The rooms in M&M are really tiny and Lower Cents isn't really near anything else."

Q "The dorms are fine. They are average dorms. **Avoid Drinker**. M&M is the best, but it's not co-ed anymore because I got caught with a girl in the shower! My fault!."

Q "Once again the dorms are hit or miss. **Some of the dorms are comfortable and clean** while others are old and dirty. The dorms to avoid are Taylor, Richards and Drinker."

Q "The dorms are **relatively small, especially the rooms**. The ability to choose has been eliminated from the registration process so you can't really choose where you want to live and where you don't."

💬 "The dorms are all decent. M & M used to be the cool dorm, but now that you can't request dorms they are all about equal. For location **I would choose M & M or Lower Cents**. Stay away from Taylor College."

💬 "The dorms are great. **None of them should be avoided**; they all have a certain something."

💬 "The decision is irrelevant since you aren't aloud to request anymore. But **I would definitely avoid the new dorm in Upper Centennial because it's all guys**. Even though you're right near sororities, those girls want nothing to do with freshmen guys."

💬 "The dorms are all pretty old, but are kept in decent condition. **M&M has the smallest rooms but is the most fun** place to live as a freshman."

💬 "You know what, as much as Lower Cents sucks, **the dorm rooms were fantastic**, and the same goes for Brodhead. If you're looking for comfort and sound sleeping quarters I definitely recommend them both. I always traveled to the crappy/fun dorms to visit my friends, and while I did spend most of my time at M&M freshman year, I can definitely tell you it was nice to go back to the serenity of Cents once in a while."

💬 "**Definitely request M&M**. It's close to the Hill, so you don't have to walk far during pledging or far to fraternity parties."

💬 "**M&M is a dumpy dorm** with closet-sized rooms, but it's the closest to the Hill, where all of the fraternities are, so it's a desirable place to live."

Q "I loved my dorm last year. I lived in Lower Cents, which is an all-freshman quad behind Taylor Gym. We had our own little grassy lot and a sand volleyball court, which was used in absolutely all weather! There were 6 dorms in our quad, each with about 45 residents, and each with a kitchen and a lounge. We were right next to the Rathbone dining hall and Taylor Gym. But the other dorms are good too. **Taylor Dorm is the substance-free**, quiet dorm. Dravo, Richards, and Drinker are nice dorms with bigger rooms but they're up the hill a little and sometimes it's a pain to walk up the stairs to get to them."

Q "The dorms are fairly typical, each a bit different in terms of rooms, number of roommates and communal bathrooms. **M&M is a popular one,** with Dravo and Lower Cents coming in close second."

The College Prowler Take On...
Campus Housing

It seems that freshmen have fond feelings for whichever dorm they wind up in. M & M has long been the most popular freshman dorm. Despite its relative age, outdated furniture and small rooms, its close proximity to the Hill makes it the number one choice of many incoming students. Dravo is usually a close second. Lower Cents has seen a dramatic increase in popularity over the last few years, due to its status as the newest dormitory which also offers the only floor of co-ed housing (that distinction used to belong to M & M) and the easiest walk to classes. The quad (Richards, Dravo and Drinker) is also a popular area to live, but can be a bit out of the way for some students, though the three dorms tend to foster a real sense of solidarity and dorm pride among its denizens. Since the admissions office has removed the option of choosing where one lives as a freshman, it doesn't make much of a difference where you reside; chances are you'll have a great time and bond with your hallmates anyway.

After freshman year, many sophomores will move into the fraternity and sorority houses they pledged. Fraternity men generally live in their house through graduation, although a decent percentage elect to live off-campus senior year. Sorority women live in their house during sophomore and junior years, and just about every sorority girl will move off-campus senior year, as there is not enough space in sorority houses for everyone and girls are usually tired of living with 60 other girls by their senior year anyway. The cost of living in a fraternity or sorority is comparable to living in the dorms, albeit slightly more expensive with parlor and social fees. Other popular on-campus housing includes Sayre Park and brand new Campus Square, but dorms will always play second fiddle as long as fraternities are still around.

The College Prowler™ Grade on
Campus Housing: B+

A high Campus Housing grade indicates that dorms are clean, well-maintained, and spacious. Other determining factors include variety of dorms, proximity to classes, and social atmosphere.

Off-Campus Housing

The Lowdown On...
Off-Campus Housing

Undergrads in Off-Campus Housing:
26%

Average Rent for a Studio:
$450/month

Average Rent for a 1BR:
$500/month

Average Rent for a 2BR:
$600/month

Average Rent for a 4BR:
$850/month

Popular Areas:
Hillside Avenue, 5th Street, Packer Avenue

For Assistance Contact:
Talk to upperclassmen, visit students who are presently living in the house you want to rent, check ads in the school newspaper, The Brown and White.

Additional information can be found at http://www3.lehigh.edu/studentlife/offcampus.asp such as a roommate forum, off-campus listings, and a guide to off-campus living

Best Time to Look for a Place
During first semester, as most leases begin June 1

Students Speak Out On...
Off-Campus Housing

"Housing is very easy off-campus, but the best houses are taken early and usually handed down through fraternities and sororities. Most people will be living in their frat and sorority house until senior year anyway."

Q "**Off-campus housing is very convenient**, but if you are in a sorority or fraternity you don't live off campus until senior year, and most of Lehigh is Greek."

Q "Off-campus housing is convenient and **costs approximately the same** as on campus housing. It is easy to find and live in."

Q "I have heard nightmare stories about some landlords. **I think living in a Greek house**, Campus Square or Sayre Park is a better option for sophomores or juniors."

Q "After freshman year you should be in a fraternity or sorority, otherwise Lehigh isn't the place for you. If, however, you are not in the Greek system, **most people live on campus** until senior year, and there is plenty of off-campus housing for everyone."

Q "It's pretty easy to get an off-campus house, and the majority of the houses are located extremely close to campus. I think **it's worth it to move off-campus**, unless you are in the Greek system which means you are living in your house until your senior year, and then you generally move off-campus."

Q "Off-campus housing is cheap and dirty with a few exceptions. **It's a must for senior year** since you're so close to the bars, unless you are lazy and want your house cleaned by pledges."

Q "**Off-campus housing is so close** to campus, that it's basically the same as on campus housing."

Q "It is definitely worth it sophomore year and beyond, but **make sure you live with people you like**."

Q "**It's extremely worth it** to live off-campus. It's very close to campus anyway, it's cheap and a lot of fun.'"

Q "Finding a house off campus was easy, but you have to plan it at least a year ahead of time, because **houses fill up quickly**."

Q "Is off-campus housing convenient? Yes. Is it worth it? Depends on what you mean. If your idea of worth involves dealing with a slumlord who's constantly trying to gouge you for money, and never being able to find parking, but always having a place to throw your own party, than yes. If you prefer to skip the renter's nightmare, than I suggest you go to someone else's **house parties**."

Q "Sororities and fraternities are on-campus at Lehigh, and this is an awesome housing option. It's a great chance to live with all of your friends and have tons of other cool people in walking distance. But **off-campus housing is really cheap** and a few streets are nearly all Lehigh kids, which makes it a lot of fun."

Q "**Off campus housing is available**, as is a lottery for on campus housing for students who do not join a fraternity or sorority. If students join a fraternity or sorority they can live in their fraternity or sorority house, which I would recommend for the bonding experience."

The College Prowler Take On...
Off-Campus Housing

Off-campus housing is abundant, although many of the best houses are handed down through their respective fraternities and sororities each year. Sorority girls often have to sign their leases more than two years in advance during their sophomore year to make sure they get the house they want. Fraternity men aren't as picky and tend to wind up with disgusting houses, but it seldom matters as many of them will have lived in relative filth and squalor during their residence in their fraternities. A small number of non-Greek students take the off-campus plunge right after freshman year and are usually pleased with the freedom and responsibility of taking care of your own house.

However, most Lehigh students who move off-campus will do so senior year, and are almost always happy with the decision. The three main bars are all off-campus, and Leon's is a two-minute walk from many houses. Most seniors will agree that it's much more convenient to leave the bars and crash at their off-campus houses than to wait for T.R.A.C.S. or figure out a way to get a ride up the Hill. There aren't too many worse experiences at Lehigh than leaving Leon's after it closes at 2 a.m. and suffering the indignity of walking back up to your fraternity house because no one is sober enough to drive. Of course, there are plenty of advantages to living in a fraternity as well, which is why a decent amount of fraternity men continue living there during senior year. As a fraternity man, the decision to move off-campus will ultimately be decided amongst your group of friends. Off-campus housing is cheap (remember, it is Bethlehem after all), convenient and a lot of fun as many seniors live very close to each other.

The College Prowler™ Grade on
Off-Campus Housing: B

A high grade in Off-Campus Housing indicates that apartments are of high quality, close to campus, affordable, and easy to secure.

Diversity

The Lowdown On...
Diversity

American Indian:
0%

Asian or Pacific Islander:
6%

African American:
3%

Hispanic:
3%

White:
85%

International:
3%

Unknown:
0%

Out of State:
69%

Most Popular Religions
Catholicism, Judaism. There are a sizable amount of students who attend church at Packer Chapel on Sundays; likewise many Jewish students attend synagogue on holy days.

Political Activity
Lehigh has a reputation as a fairly conservative campus, which isn't surprising given the sheer amount of wealth many of the students come from. As a result, there is a good deal of political apathy, and while there are students who get more involved in politics and causes, they are in the minority and seldom seen.

Gay Tolerance
The campus is accepting of the gay community, but you wouldn't know it by looking at the students. At such a homogenized school, any students considering coming out would probably be better off elsewhere.

Economic Status
Again, it's no secret that Lehigh students generally come from a lot of money. Lehigh may as well adopt Audi's A4 as the official school car.

Minority Clubs
The Umoja House, which is dedicated to exploring African American and Hispanic traditions, students in the Umoja House take an active role in planning a variety of social, cultural and educational programs focused on learning more about these cultures.

Students Speak Out On...
Diversity

> "The campus isn't diverse at all. Most students come from the same background, the east coast, and same ethnic group. However, each student has different interests, which makes our campus diverse in a different sense."

Q "Our campus is **not very diverse**; if you're looking for an upper-class white school this is the place to be."

Q "I'll break it down for you: Lehigh has about **5000 white kids and 10 black kids.**"

Q "The campus is **not diverse** at all. There's been a push on campus for more diversity, but I am still waiting to see that happen."

Q **"It's become a lot more diverse** since my freshmen year. Lehigh is making a huge effort to diversify the school."

Q "Lehigh is about as **diverse as the crowd at a Green Bay Packers game** minus the players on the field."

Q "There's **plenty of diversity**. Let's see…there's white people, white Protestants, white Jews and white Catholics. That's about it."

Q **"There's no diversity at all,** so don't look for it. They may trick you with the few organizations they have floating around, but it's just so that they can say they have them."

Q "Campus is not diverse at all. It's too bad, **the minorities feel like outcasts**. I know because I took a diversity class. Lehigh tries to promote diversity but they don't really want it, it's just a political thing so they can receive more funding. If they were really serious about it, it would be great for the campus."

Q "**We're pretty diverse**; I think a truly diversified campus is hard to find when there are only 5,000 undergrads. I think Lehigh does its best to make the campus as racially mixed as possible."

Q "As far as diversity, there's **a fair amount of foreign students**, but its mostly a rich white school, I'm not gonna lie. When the football team has an away game there's not much diversity around campus, if you know what I mean."

Q "Lehigh is filled with rich white kids. **The guys still outnumber the girls**. And while there are minorities, they mostly stick together."

Q "If you are looking for a school in a place that offers tons of different stuff and a lot of diversity, Lehigh isn't it. I **wish I had chosen a school that was more diverse**."

The College Prowler Take On...
Diversity

Lehigh, despite its academic excellence, has a very poor track record regarding diversity. This doesn't mean that diversity is nonexistent, in fact there are a decent number of students of African-American and Asian descent, but these small groups tend to stay very close to each other, which isn't entirely surprising given Lehigh's tremendous Caucasian population. The university has made attempts to help further integrate campus; the African-American fraternity Kappa Alpha Psi was finally officially recognized by Lehigh last year, and a renovated fraternity house has been turned into the multicultural Umoja House, a residence hall in which students of all different ethnicities live together.

But Lehigh is still very much dominated by wealthy white students. The most prevalent religions are Judaism and Christianity and a huge percentage of the student body hails from Pennsylvania, New Jersey and New York, with a good number of the New Yorkers hailing from Westchester and Long Island. Despite the university's efforts, Lehigh will still likely remain a very homogenous school for a long time.

The College Prowler™ Grade on
Diversity: D+

A high grade in Diversity indicates that ethnic minorities and international students have a notable presence on campus and that students of different economic backgrounds, religious beliefs, and sexual preferences are well-represented.

Guys & Girls

The Lowdown On...
Guys & Girls

Men Undergrads:
54.7%

Women Undergrads:
45.3%

Birth Control Available?
Yes, by appointment at the Health Center with Planned Parenthood

Social Scene
Lehigh students are incredibly outgoing. As with most colleges, freshman year is the most social as everyone wants to be everyone else's friend and you're still trying to decide who you actually get along with. However, most students will eventually find a group of friends who become a second family.

Hookups or Relationships?
Lehigh students often like to say that relationships are nonexistent, which isn't entirely true. There are a fair amount of students who attempt to settle down. Many students will have at least one "significant other" throughout their four years. But for the most part, Lehigh certainly lives up to the reputation of "let's get drunk and hook-up." There are tons of hook-ups going on every weekend, and it's much easier to hook up at a fraternity party on any given weekend than to try and find that one special someone.

Best Place to Meet Guys/Girls:
Fraternities are hands-down the number one place to interact with members of the opposite sex. At the average Lehigh party, you'll find cases upon cases of beer plus assorted drinking games and outgoing coeds—what more could you want?

Top Places to Hookup:
1. Fraternity bedrooms
2. Freshman dorms
3. Leon's or off-campus houses

Dress Code
Once again, the dress code reflects students' wealth. Guys are generally clad in either Diesel jeans or Abercrombie and Polo Ralph Lauren attire; every single girl on campus owns multiple pairs of Seven jeans and wouldn't be caught dead without their Louis Vitton or Prada handbags. Both guys' and girls' styles are mostly either New York club attire or straight-up preppy.

Did You Know?
Top Places to Find Hotties:
1. Fraternity parties
2. Sorority houses
3. Off-campus bars

Students Speak Out On...
Guys & Girls

"Every year fraternity guys get really excited because the new freshmen come up to their houses, because after freshman year many girls tend to gain considerable weight. I wouldn't say we're a 'hot' school, but there's a fair share of really attractive people."

Q "I think the guys are hotter than the girls. I'm sure there are many hot girls who I've never met, but on the whole I think there are a lot **more attractive men then women**."

Q "I know its cliché, but the guys that I know are 'frat guys' - big drinkers and like to get wasted and hook-up. But most of the guys are also really chill and make great friends. As for the girls, a lot of them are definitely 'clique-y' and **girls tend to hang out with girls in their own sorority**. I have some friends in other houses, but you have to work at staying close with them."

Q "I had the privilege of being roommates with the best-looking and best Beirut player in the history of the school so I'd say yes, the men are hot. Lehigh **girls aren't exactly the hottest in the world but it could be worse**."

Q "The **boys are generally pretty preppy**; however each fraternity characterizes a different group of guys. Lehigh is represented pretty well and yes there are a few hot guys. The girls are thought to be jappy, but overall they are pretty and nice."

Q "**Guys are much better looking than the girls**. I actually feel sorry for the guys a lot of the time."

Q "Lehigh is a very **good-looking** campus."

Q "The guys vary, but for the most part they're preppy. **Most of the girls are high-maintenance**, at least the ones I hung around with."

Q "There is **pretty much one type of girl** on campus. There are not that many great-looking guys. If you're looking for love, look somewhere else, but you will sure as hell have a good time with the opposite sex while you're there."

Q "**Guys are definitely fun**! They used to be much cuter. The girls are great too; I never made better girl friends in my life."

Q "The guys are mostly **east-coast preppy frat guys**--polo shirts, flip-flops and keg stands. They know how to party and are always happy to invite girls over to share their booze. On the whole, they're not bad."

Q "The guys are hot for the most part, but most of them think they're all that, so you have to really get to know them and then you actually see how nice they can be. As far as girls go, there are lots of hot girls on campus, but like any school, there are all different types of girls. You just have to **get to know them and what they're like.**"

Q "**Well, there's a 60 to 40** guy to girl ratio so for us the odds are good! There are actually a lot of pretty good-looking guys here. I brought a lot of Lehigh pictures home over winter break and all of my high school friends were like ... 'Omigosh! Every guy in these pics is so hot!' But you don't notice it so much when they're your friends. I love the people here. Everyone seems so nice and sincere. They're just REAL... it's hard to find the fake ones."

Q "I **don't care for frat guys much.** They think they are the greatest thing since the light bulb."

Q "I'd say there's a decent amount of the student body that's good-looking; unfortunately, there are also a **lot of people** that think they're better looking than they really are."

Q "There are **LOTS of hot guys on campus**, but a lot of them are obsessed with beer and getting laid. There are some good ones, you just have to be on the lookout for the nice boys! Some of the girls are really snobby. You know, the stereotypical sorority types. But again, you'll find your niche."

Q "Lehigh is a relatively **homogenous school with most students coming from New York**, New Jersey and Pennsylvania. Lehigh tends to preach diversity to prospective students on tours and info sessions, but as in any situation, many tend to stick with their own social groups."

The College Prowler Take On...
Guys & Girls

Let's get one thing straight: Lehigh is a very good-looking campus. Almost everyone agrees that there are plenty of attractive guys, and while there may not be quite as many hot girls as there are guys, there are still a decent amount. Most girls agree that the guys are hot, and although some of them have big egos, many of them are very friendly and outgoing. The guys are mostly pretty boys and preppies. Guys are a little more reluctant to call the girls hot, but the hesitation is borne out of many girls' personalities. While there are a lot of chill, fun girls, the hotter ones tend to be very bitchy and either already have boyfriends or some kind of borderline personality disorder or both. As a result, the guys drink very heavily and tend to hook-up with less attractive girls much to the enjoyment of their friends, who will not hesitate to make fun of them relentlessly the next morning.

Due to the sheer volume of drinking that occurs at Lehigh, there is a huge number of random drunken hook-ups on any given night. Anytime you mix a group of horny co-eds and provide gallons of beer, there's going to be drunken hooking-up. Inhibitions disappear, standards vanish and beer goggles ensue. Though some students will develop relationships and even fall in love, Lehigh is not much of a dating school. The lucky few who do find that special someone often become completely involved in their relationships, effectively shutting out their friends and shunning parties. Doing so is a huge social mistake, which is why most people who do have significant others will do their best to balance their relationship, their friends, schoolwork and social lives. It may sound tricky, but it's actually a lot easier than it seems. Many students will probably have at least one real relationship during their four years, but at its heart Lehigh has always had a random hook-up, one-night stand social atmosphere.

The College Prowler™ Grade on Guys: B+

A high grade for Guys indicates that the male population on campus is attractive, smart, friendly, and engaging, and that the school has a decent ratio of guys to girls.

The College Prowler™ Grade on Girls: B

A high grade for Girls not only implies that the women on campus are attractive, smart, friendly, and engaging, but also that there is a fair ratio of girls to guys.

Athletics

The Lowdown On...
Athletics

Athletic Division:
Lehigh sponsors 25 varsity sports competing at the NCAA Division I level (I-AA for football). Lehigh's varsity athletic teams compete in the Patriot League and the Eastern Intercollegiate Wrestling Association (EIWA).

Conference:
Patriot League

Men's Varsity Sports:
Baseball
Basketball
Cross Country
Football
Golf
Lacrosse
Soccer
Swimming & Diving
Tennis
Indoor Track & Field
Outdoor Track & Field
Wrestling

Women's Varsity Sports:
Basketball
Crew
Cross Country
Field Hockey
Golf
Lacrosse
Soccer
Softball
Swimming & Diving
Tennis
Indoor Track & Field
Outdoor Track & Field
Volleyball

Club Sports:
Men's Crew
Ice Hockey
Bowling
Crew
Equestrian
Frisbee
Golf
Gymnastics
Ice Hockey B
Lacrosse (Men)
Lacrosse (Women)
Mountain Biking
Rifle
Rugby (Men)
Rugby (Women)
Running
Sailing
Ski
Soccer
Tae-Kwon-Do
Tennis
Volleyball

Intramurals:
Basketball
Flag Football
Indoor Soccer
Soccer
Softball
Turkey Trot
Volleyball

Athletic Fields
Goodman Stadium
Stabler Arena

School Mascot
Mountain Hawk

Getting Tickets
Students do not need tickets to attend Lehigh sporting events. All students have to do is flash their ID in order to get in to the football games.

Most Popular Sports
Lehigh football and wrestling are both incredibly popular among townies and throughout the Lehigh Valley. Students are mostly apathetic towards their sports teams.

Overlooked Teams
Given that students barely pay attention to athletics, even if there were teams that were considered overlooked, they still wouldn't bother paying attention to them.

Best Place to Take a Walk
Goodman Campus

Gyms/Facilities

Taylor Gym
The Welch Fitness Center and Racquet Sports Complex, located in Taylor Gymnasium, is a multi-dimensional facility intended for use by students, faculty, and staff. The center provides the university community the opportunity to improve their health and physical fitness through the use of the center's "state of the art" equipment and programs.

Did You Know?
- The year 2004 marked the 140th meeting of the Lehigh-Lafayette football game, college football's **most played rivalry.**

- There are **5,480 seats** available in Stabler Arena.

Students Speak Out On...
Athletics

> "Varsity sports are pretty big on campus given the small student body. Football games tend to be huge (tailgates) and basketball and wrestling get a good showing also. IM sports are participated in by every fraternity and freshman halls so you can imagine the intensity."

Q "Although I do not participate, **sports are big** and there is a lot of Lehigh spirit."

Q "**Varsity sports are big,** but I think it's great that the athletes are just like everyone else when in class and when people go out at night."

Q "Varsity football is almost **half as big as the tailgate parties** preceding it. Most people are too drunk by 12:00 in the afternoon to attend the games. The other sports do not get too many spectators but wrestling is very popular."

Q "**Varsity sports are not that big**. People go to the football games and big events, but attendance is not like it is at the Big 10 or larger schools. There are intramural sports, which many people actively participate in."

Q "Lehigh has **great school spirit.** From football to soccer, all the sports teams draw crowds. IM sports are a lot of fun, and my sorority is joining IM flag football this semester."

"**Football and wrestling are fairly big**. Intramural softball is fun to play drunk and IM soccer is for those who don't smoke. IM basketball is unfairly ruled by one team every year."

"Despite my own house's **lack of participation,** other people participate in IM sports enthusiastically and have a great time doing it."

"I think we have a **lot of school spirit** considering Lehigh's a relatively small school."

"**Tailgates and playing Beirut are the biggest athletic events on campus**. Then there is Lehigh-Lafayette weekend, but that is not so much a sport as an institution."

"Do not let them kid you. If you are an athlete and you play anything other than football or wrestling, then it's not really worth it. If you ask me, there are major problems with the Lehigh Athletic Department and there always seems to be difficulties with their coaching staff, no matter what the sport. Please talk to other athletes about the team before you join. Do not be wooed by recruiting trips. I'd say that there are hardly any special benefits for being a Lehigh Athlete (Oh, there's one; you get to choose your classes before anyone else). **IM sports, on the other hand, are pretty chill and well worth your time**."

"Our upper campus consists of mostly all the sports fields and facilities. **Football is huge in the fall**. The team has done well these last couple years so more and more fans are attracted to the already huge crowd that accumulates at Goodman Stadium. I must add that the biggest rivalry in football history, Lehigh vs. Lafayette is an experience that you will never forget! The parties start Monday for the following Saturday's game! It's crazy!."

Q "**Varsity sports are fairly big.** Football is major, and almost everyone on campus goes to all the home games and tailgates that take up the grassy area at the field. The games are free for students. I love our big games like Lehigh/Lafayette (our rival) and the Championships. They are so much fun and Lehigh football ALWAYS wins. We also have an unbelievable wrestling squad who are always ranked nationally. A lot of students watch their matches. And I see some friends at the track meets too. But I would say IM sports are even bigger than the varsity. I was on the IM volleyball and indoor soccer teams which was a ton of fun. The guys get really into it. Practically the whole school watches or plays IM sports."

Q "The only varsity of sports of note here are **football and wrestling, both are huge** though. IM sports are fairly involved - most dorms, fraternities, sororities, and even off-campus houses field teams...There's a lot of sports at the club level as well, if you're looking for something a little more competitive."

Q "Lehigh football and **perhaps soccer will attract some students**. Though Lehigh cannot be compared to a Big Ten school as far as sports are concerned, games are a great time if attendance is decent, and of course if there's a win!."

The College Prowler Take On...
Athletics

Lehigh's greatest athletic tradition is waking up at 8 a.m. on Saturday mornings and getting wasted before home football games. Kidding aside, morning cocktails and tailgates are some of the most popular events during the whole school year. Fraternities will go around their house, sorority houses and freshman dorms with pots and pans to wake everyone up, and as difficult as it may be to wake up that early on a Saturday after a long night of boozing, tailgates usually sees a very impressive turnout. It's hard to pass up the exuberance of drinking outside the football stadium on a beautiful sunny day as the entire campus walks around to each fraternity's set-up in search of barbequed food and beer, as the police just stand back and watch. Few attend the actual football game, which is unfortunate given the team's remarkable success during the regular season over the last few years. Wrestling is the other insanely popular sport at Lehigh, although it's more revered by alumni and the town of Bethlehem. In fact, townies are probably more into the football and wrestling teams than the student body is, which is not surprising given the lack of nearby professional sports teams. The wrestling team is consistently ranked in the top ten in the country, and Lehigh boasted the #1 wrestler in the country last year.

Intramural sports are wildly popular as it allows the more casual athletes to participate in a wide variety of sports. Freshman teams are made up of halls in the dormitories and upperclass teams are made up of fraternity against fraternity and sorority against sorority. In the fall, students play soccer, followed by indoor soccer, volleyball and basketball in the winter and softball and flag football in the spring. There was even an organized IM Beirut league between fraternities a few years ago, and it was very popular at first but not enough houses knew about it, and it eventually dissipated. Winning intramural sports gives fraternities bragging rights and bolsters a sense of pride and athleticism. Most students tend to get much more involved in intramurals than Lehigh's sports teams.

The College Prowler™ Grade on
Athletics: B+

A high grade in Athletics indicates that students have school spirit, that sports programs are respected, that games are well-attended, and that intramurals are a prominent part of student life.

Nightlife

The Lowdown On...
Nightlife

Club and Bar Prowler: Popular Nightlife Spots!

The "Big Three" (Leon's, McGrady's, The Ho) completely dominate Lehigh's bar scene, and not because any of them are particularly amazing, but rather that they are the most convenient. Most 21-year-olds live off-campus as it is, and Leon's is a block away from a good majority of houses. McGrady's and the Ho are a quick car ride away, but be careful about driving drunk, Bethlehem police are always just around the corner . The Funhouse, which was actually voted one of the top 20 dive bars in Stuff Magazine, and the Happy Tap are alternatives, but most students stay away because both are extremely dive and are populated with townies. The Copperhead Grill and Our Beer Belly's are fun and enable students to take a break from the scene, but also happen to be a car ride away and very rarely do you find a Lehigh student eager to be the designated driver.

Copperhead Grille

Address: 5737 Route 378, Bethlehem

Phone: (610) 282-4600

The Copperhead is also a fairly new bar, and probably the closest thing Bethlehem has to a club. The bar has karaoke Tuesdays, a DJ on Wednesdays and Fridays and a band on Saturdays. It's also the biggest bar in the area and has become very popular with Lehigh seniors as a venue for bi-monthly "Senior Nights." Copperhead's main drawback is that it's a trek from campus, and even the most daring drunk drivers would do well to avoid taking the risk.

The Funhouse

Address: 5 E. 4th Street, South Side Bethlehem

Phone: (610) 868-5311

As previously mentioned, the Funhouse appeared in Stuff Magazine's 20 biggest dive bars in the country. Upon entering, it will become blatantly apparent why it was honored with such a distinction. The drink selection is considerably limited, the bar is small and dingy and about the only saving grace is that they have an area sectioned off for musical acts to perform. The Funhouse can be an alternative to the typical Leon's/McGrady's bar scene, but it must be taken in small doses.

The Happy Tap

Address: 601 E. 4th Street, South Side Bethlehem

Phone: (610) 865-2790

If possible, the Happy Tap may be even more of a dive than the Funhouse, although it does have a fair amount of character, as most dive bars do. The Tap is probably the least popular of all the bars among Lehigh students, but it's incredibly cheap and, like the Funhouse, a good alternative to the normal scene.

J.P. McGrady's Pub

Address: 117 E. 3rd Street, South Side Bethlehem

Phone: (610) 868-8925

McGrady's has 40 beers on tap and has $3 pitchers of Miller Light on select nights. They also have karaoke on Wednesday nights. The walls are covered with old-fashioned beer signs and it has a very all-American appeal to it. Even the bathroom has a trough instead of a urinal. McGrady's has about a million times more seating then Leon's and also features two Photo Hunt machines, both of which are playable for a quarter. One aspect of the bar that's incredibly annoying is the layout; the actual bar itself juts out so much so that getting into the back seating area on a crowded night is near-impossible.

Leon's

432 E. 5th Street, Bethlehem

(610) 868-6822

Leon's has been a staple of Lehigh seniors for as long as it's been in existence. There's nothing overwhelmingly appealing about the bar, other than the fact that it's the most convenient for the majority of people living off-campus. Inside, it's fairly standard, domestic beers are $2.50, imported $3.50. It has a pool table and the all-important MegaTouch Force machine which includes the incredibly addicting Photo Hunt game, although Leon's charges an obscenely overpriced $1.00 per play. Leon's also has an outside area in the back with tables and is opened in warm weather. No one's really sure why there's a giant sandbox out on the back, but it's there and manages to add to the appeal of the bar. The bar's most popular nights are Thursdays, as they charge a $2 cover for a live DJ. Otherwise, Leon's has no particular specials to speak of.

Our Beer Belly's

Address: 25 E. East Elizabeth Ave., Bethlehem

Phone: (610) 861-8120

Beer Belly's is another solid all-around bar. The beer is cheap and the food is good, but once again, its distance from campus makes it impossible to ever become a staple.

Starter's Pub

Address: 3731 Route 378, Bethlehem

Phone: (610) 997-5454

Starters is an excellent sports bar and restaurant, but is most often frequented at dinnertime and Sunday afternoons for football. It's a fun bar, but not the kind of place one hangs out at to get absolutely smashed.

Tally Ho Tavern

Address: 205 W. 4th Street, South Side Bethlehem

Phone: (610) 865-2591

The Ho is the oldest bar in Bethlehem's South Side. There are plenty of booths as well as an excellent outdoor seating area, although it's primarily used during the day for eating. The Ho has occasional drink specials, but once again, beer is so cheap in Bethlehem that if they had any specials they'd practically be giving it away for free (besides, that job is already taken by the fraternities). The Ho also has a separate room for live musical acts and another separate game room with pool tables and arcade games, as well as a $0.25 Photo Hunt machine. The Ho has seen its popularity decline somewhat, especially with the opening of McGrady's, but the bar's popular enough and has been such a mainstay that it won't be going anywhere for a long time.

Your Welcome Inn
Address: 325 S. New Street, South Side Bethlehem
Phone: (610) 868-8887

Your Welcome Inn is an absolute piece of garbage. The only Lehigh students who bother going are freshmen, since they can't get in anywhere else. No one's really sure why this bar continues to exist.

Other Places to Check Out:

Steelgaarden (the bar located below Brew Works)

Bars Close At:

2 a.m.

Primary Areas with Nightlife:

3rd Street, 4th Street, 5th Street

Cheapest Place to Get a Drink:

The three main bars are all priced about the same.

Favorite Drinking Games:

Beirut
Card Games
Century Club
Scud
Flip Cup
Quarters
Power Hour

Student Favorites

Leon's, McGrady's, The Tally Ho

Useful Resources for Nightlife

www.Lehighlive.com

What to Do if You're Not 21

Attend fraternity parties, drink in your dorm room

Local Specialties

There are no specialty drinks, although Pennsylvania residents enjoy and are very proud of Yuengling, as it's brewed in their home state.

Club Crawler

Sadly, there are no clubs in Bethlehem. And if there were, they'd be incredibly out of place.

Organization Parties

The only organizational parties to speak of are the events orchestrated by the senior class leaders. There is a Senior Night party every other week, which usually entails a $5 cover. The money goes towards Senior Week down at the beach in May, right before graduation.

Frats

See the Greek Section!

Students Speak Out On...
Nightlife

> "The parties on campus are what this school is all about. Our fraternity life is unparalleled by any school in the nation. The best bars off-campus are Leon's, JP McGrady's, and the Ho."

Q "The social scene at Lehigh **revolves around fraternity life**, so most of the partying is done on the Hill. Some people think it gets old, but I don't agree."

Q "The parties on campus are always inviting and exciting to freshman. **I remember being overwhelmed** but it is easy to find where you fit in as well as where you benefit from the most."

Q "**Lehigh has a great party scene** - there is always something going on at different fraternities on the hill. Everything is really laid back too. The bars off-campus are strict with IDs, though a lot of juniors and seniors end up there at the end of the night."

Q "**The parties on campus are amazing**. Lehigh has the best fraternity scene in the country. The bars are rarely visited by anyone other than seniors or young girls looking to hook-up."

Q "**Parties on campus are great.** The bars are fun if you go to the right ones. You need to hit up the correct bars on the correct nights for a good time. The local favorites are J.P. McGrady's, The Tally Ho and Leon's."

Q "**The parties are very good.** There isn't really a bar/club scene here. The bars are really for the seniors."

Q "The Hill used to be a lot of fun. Now the cops tend to break parties up and most events are registered and get quite crowded. Parties off-campus are great for seniors. Leon's is a great bar when the weather is nice and if you want to dance. The Funhouse has bands weekly and pool. McGrady's can get a **little too crowded.**"

Q "I love the parties on campus. It's very comfortable because you know a lot of people and therefore feel safe. The bars off-campus, though limited, **are a lot of fun.** They are inexpensive and low-key."

Q "Parties are hit or miss. It depends on the house and the night and what sorority is hanging out, etc. Leon's is best for random fun at 1:30 a.m., **McGrady's is great for Tuesday nights** and the Ho is good for Live Bands and semi-civilized nights. Only go to the Funhouse for blackout, hook-up-with-fat-townie nights."

Q "The parties were incredible when I was a freshman, however they have tamed down substantially, although every now and then things return to the glory days of partying. The Ho is good for senior night, Leon's is great for dancing, and **MacGrady's is basically the place to be every night** if you don't want to run into townies and you want to be more laid back."

Q "**The parties on campus are fun** and are mostly focused on binge drinking and frequent random hookups. Leon's, The Tally-Ho and McGrady's are the good off-campus bars."

Q "You hear it every year: **'Parties on campus aren't what they used to be.'** And it's true. I'm too far removed from the scene to tell you whether someone new would have fun or not, however, my best friend's little sister was a freshman last year, and she had a blast, so maybe it's just a matter of being jaded. McGrady's has become the new Leon's: Everyone and their mom parties there and its pretty much always packed party nights Wed.-Sat. The Ho is still cool, and they often have worthy entertainment. My fave is and always will be The Funhouse. Hardly any of the standard Lehigh Cliques go there, they have excellent entertainment, and the bar owner, Tina, is wonderful. If you're looking for clubs you may as well just save the energy and drive into Philly or NYC if you want to dance."

Q "**Again, campus life is awesome** for a reason: There is not too much going on outside of campus. The Ho is a good happy hour bar, and Leon's is the ultimate neighborhood spot - the bartender usually knows everyone's name by the middle of first semester. In fact, it sometimes feels more like a house party than a bar. But that's what makes Lehigh great."

Q "Parties on campus are either on the Hill where all of the fraternity houses are located or off-campus at students' homes. **There are three bars to choose from**, The Tally Ho, Leon's or McGrady's. All are pretty divey and relatively small, but everything is what you make of it, which at Lehigh is usually a good time. The club scene at Lehigh is really lacking, as there are no clubs."

The College Prowler Take On...
Nightlife

Fraternities dominate the social scene from freshman through junior year, as many students will probably spend more hours playing Beirut than in class or the library. A big reason for the tremendous popularity of the Hill is because there just aren't many other options for underage students. The local bars card very hard; it's not unusual to hear of a Lehigh student who got arrested over the weekend trying to use a fake ID at Leon's. At times it seems that the local Bethlehem bars card harder than most places in New York City. As such, incoming freshman better get used to lots of Beirut quickly.

Of course some people complain that playing Beirut every night gets tedious, which is true for just about anything, but those students who are over 21 mix things up by going to the local bars. There are three main drinking establishments that students tend to choose; the aforementioned Tally Ho, McGrady's, and Leon's. McGrady's just opened in 2002 and gained popularity very quickly, due to good deals and the fact that there was finally an alternative to the Ho and Leon's, but Leon's has always been a mainstay. Its prime location to off-campus housing and cheap prices makes it a must-visit every weekend night. There are two other seldom-visited dive bars in the area, the Happy Tap and the Funhouse. The Funhouse was actually featured in Maxim's 20 biggest dive bars in America and occasionally features live music, so it can be a refreshing alternative. On any given weekend night there are also a fair number of free off-campus parties on Hillside Avenue, but are usually exclusive to either seniors or members of whichever fraternity or sorority that is scheduled to party there. It's much more inviting (and safer) for freshmen to wander the Hill in search of nightlife rather than off-campus.

The College Prowler™ Grade on
Nightlife: C+

A high grade in Nightlife indicates that there are many bars and clubs in the area that are easily accessible and affordable. Other determining factors include the number of options for the under-21 crowd and the prevalence of house parties.

Greek Life

The Lowdown On...
Greek Life

Number of Fraternities:
23

Number of Sororities:
9

Percent of Undergrad Men in Fraternities:
40%

Percent of Undergrad Women in Sororities:
40%

Fraternities on Campus:
Alpha Chi Rho (Crow), Alpha Sigma Phi (Alpha Sig), Alpha Tau Omega (ATO), Beta Theta Pi (Beta), Chi Phi, Chi Psi, Delta Phi (D Phi), Delta Sigma Phi (Delta Sig), Delta Tau Delta (Delts), Delta Upsilon (DU), Kappa Alpha (KA), Kappa Sigma (Kappa Sig), Lambda Chi Alpha (Lambda Chi), Phi Gamma Delta (Fiji), Phi Kappa Theta (Phi Kap), Phi Sigma Kappa (Phi Sig), Psi Upsilon (Psi U), Sigma Alpha Mu (Sammy), Sigma Chi, Sigma Phi Epsilon (Sig Ep), Theta Chi, Theta Delta Chi (Theta Delt), Theta Xi

Sororities on Campus:
Alpha Chi Omega (A Chi O), Alpha Gamma Delta (Alpha Gam), Alpha Omicron Pi (A O Pi), Alpha Phi, Chi Omega (Chi O), Delta Gamma (DG), Gamma Phi Beta (Gamma Phi), Kappa Alpha Theta (Theta), Pi Beta Phi (Pi Phi)

Other Greek Organizations
Interfraternity Council
Panhellenic Council

Multicultural Colonies:
Kappa Alpha Psi

Did You Know?

Every April, **the newly initiated members** of all of the fraternities and sororities square off in various competitions during Greek Week.

Students Speak Out On...
Greek Life

> "I would say it dominates the social scene. I can't really speak for non-Greeks, but mostly all my friends are in houses and when I go out, it's almost always to a fraternity party. I would tell people to definitely rush if they come to Lehigh. It's a huge part of my life at Lehigh."

- "Greek life dominates all at Lehigh."

- "Greek life is **extremely dominant!** At times it seems to me that there isn't much going on outside of being Greek. It provides such a great social life and friends."

- "**Yes, Greek life dominates** the social scene. The school is doing its best to get rid of it, but the Greeks are too strong and eradication will probably never happen."

- "**Greek life is pretty big;** while it doesn't dominate an individual's social life, the on-campus parties are all in fraternity houses and are for the most part held with sororities. That is not to say that your life will suck if you aren't Greek, it will be the same, but in terms of campus stuff, the Greek system is extremely strong. I think something like 40% of students are Greek."

- "**Greek life is decreasing**, but it still dominates the social scene. However, all fraternity parties are open so anyone can come. It is also nice to be part of Greek life beyond the social aspects."

Q "I don't think Greek life dominates the social scene as much as other people might. I have been to **a lot of parties that do not just have sorority girls and fraternity guys** there. And once you move off-campus those lines blur and everyone just goes to the bar and hangs out. Joining a sorority was one of the best things I could have done. I have made incredible friends that I wouldn't trade for the world. However, I feel that I am not defined by my sorority and who my house hangs out with."

Q "**Greek Life is active** and varies a lot by house to house, although recent attempts by the school to kill it have worked well and have left frat parties a mere shadow of their former selves.'"

Q "**The social scene completely revolves around Greek life**. There are only a few bars around, so there are tons of frat parties every night. If you don't think that you are interested in going Greek, then Lehigh is not the right place for you."

Q "While **Greek life used to dominate** the social scene, it has become less and less necessary to maintain an active and fun social life. It is however, the main focal point of the party scene for underclassmen."

Q "**Greek life is the social scene.** If you don't join a house your freshman year, you might as well transfer to another school because you will have no social life."

Q "There is nothing else to do in Bethlehem, so **life becomes one giant frat party**. I didn't see anything wrong with that. Others might. It's just the way it is. That's why the alumni have been getting pissed off, because the administration keeps pulling the plug on so many of them. It's tradition and it's what we believe in."

Q "Basically the entire campus is Greek. It's fun if you like that kind of thing. It probably sucks if you're not included and you want to be. **It's basically one big social circle** where everyone knows everyone."

Q "**Greek life is awesome.** If you're looking to join a fraternity or sorority, this is the school to go to. Greek life certainly dominates the social scene, with Beirut tournaments, Greek-sponsored off-campus parties, dance parties etc. You can find a frat party every single day of the week. This school knows how to party!"

Q "Ahhh ... Greek Life ... I would say **it plays a pretty big role with the social scene**. You can find a party on any Tuesday, Wednesday, Thursday, Friday and Saturday night. At a typical party, music will be playing, some people will be dancing, and someone will always be playing Beirut. However, there are also some hot parties in off-campus houses that are not associated with Greek Life. I would say the majority of the campus does rush but there are still a good amount of people who don't. Whatever you decide to do, you'll always be welcome anywhere. Another great thing about Lehigh is that you never have to pay ... free beer!."

Q "**Greek life is very prominent** at Lehigh. It is a major part of the social scene and a great way to meet people."

The College Prowler Take On...
Greek Life

The Greek scene is Lehigh's bread and butter. While the school may not want to admit it, Lehigh students drink and party harder than just about anyone. The administration has taken a number of steps in trying to curb binge drinking and unregistered parties over the last decade or so, and many Lehigh alumni tend to return to the school and claim the social scene is nothing compared to what it once was when they were students, but current students are almost always one step ahead and clever enough to avoid having their fun completely destroyed. All of Lehigh's fraternities are located on the Hill, and preside authoritatively over the rest of campus. The fraternity scene is still the be-all end-all for partying. On top of that, all parties are free, including off-campus parties. People have toyed with the idea of charging at the door, but unless every house started doing it, the idea would never catch on because people would always gravitate towards the free house parties. You can conceivably go all four years at Lehigh without spending a dime on beer. Of course, all fraternity members pay social (some members more than drink what they pay for) and chances are you're gonna hit up the bar scene at some point or another, but compared to fraternities and off-campus parties at other schools that charge $5 for admittance and a 12-ounce Solo cup, Lehigh is cheap and the beer is constantly flowing. For kids who are vehemently anti-Greek, Lehigh is not the school to attend. Greek life isn't for everyone, but those who don't join a Greek organization really don't get the full Lehigh "experience."

Of course, there are some negative aspects to being Greek, one being that people often get stereotyped (pretty boys, druggies, athletes, hippies) depending on which house they're in; another the high school cliquey aspect inherent in separating groups of people into houses, some of which are deemed cool and hot and others as losers and ugly; as well as the fact that almost everyone knows your business unless you are incredibly shady, but otherwise being in a fraternity or sorority at Lehigh is like no other experience in the world.

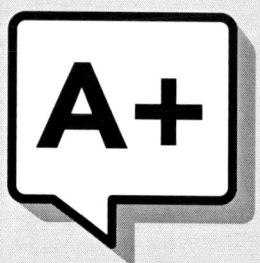

The College Prowler™ Grade on
Greek Life: A+

A high grade in Greek Life indicates that sororities and fraternities are not only present, but also active on campus. Other determining factors include the variety of houses available and the respect the Greek community receives from the rest of the campus.

Drug Scene

The Lowdown On...
Drug Scene

Most Prevalent Drugs on Campus:
Marijuana
Adderall
Cocaine
Mushrooms

Liquor-Related Referrals:
106

Liquor-Related Arrests:
49

Drug-Related Referrals:
18

Drug-Related Arrests:
12

Drug Counseling Programs
Lehigh University Health Center
(610) 758-3870

Services: alcohol assessment services, short-term counseling, alcohol-related literature

Students Speak Out On...
Drug Scene

> "I wouldn't say there's a huge drug scene, but every type of drug you could possibly think of is at Lehigh. If that's not your thing it's very easy to not be around drugs."

Q "I don't think the scene is rampant, but I'm sure **if you wanted some sort of drug you could find it**."

Q "**Pot is pretty big** and widely used. As for other drugs, even though they are around, people keep them pretty much quiet."

Q "I like drugs, especially marijuana and mushrooms. **You can find anything you want on campus**. I've actually never run into heroin but I'm sure some kids did it."

Q "**It's not that bad here.** The more the school cracks down on alcohol, though, the more drugs roll in."

Q "**Lehigh should chill with the crackdown on drinking**. Otherwise kids are going to start smoking crack."

Q "Although I do not take part in it, **I know that drugs are prevalent** on our campus."

Q "**Pot is big,** but it also is everywhere. And I think the cocaine problems are dying down a little."

Q "You can find people who do anything if you want it. **Drug use isn't very blatant** except for pot."

Q "The scene is smaller than at most schools, I think. You have the standards: **Marijuana and a bit of cocaine.** You probably see more prescription pain killers than anything else."

Q "There **used to be a lot more drug use on campus**. It has dropped significantly in the past three years."

Q "**Whatever, drugs are everywhere**. I've seen a few kids drop out because of them, and others strive because of them. If you're going to talk about drugs, how about we talk about them all? Did you know that the second most prescribed drug on campus is Paxil? It's true. So would I rather have a few potheads running around or a bunch of morons in a 'box'? I don't know."

Q "**There are plenty of pot-smokers** and dabblers in other things at Lehigh. Pretty much all my friends smoke weed. Pot is everywhere and just as easy to get as a beer. If you want anything stronger than that, you have to look a little harder."

Q "The drug scene, as at any other school, can be **found if one would like to find it**."

The College Prowler Take On...
Drug Scene

There's no college in America that doesn't have its fair share of kids who smoke weed. College has always been known as a time to try new things, and many students will experiment with drugs at some point or another if they haven't already. That being said, Lehigh's drug scene is really no more prevalent than at any other school. Pot is almost always available as long as you know the right people, although the police are far more attuned to the drug scene that many students realize and there has been a significant number of drug-related arrests over the past few years.

On top of the availability of pot, there is also a fairly startling amount of prescription drug abuse. It is not uncommon for students to pop pill after pill of adderall during midterms and finals, and plenty of students use speed on a daily basis for mere homework assignments. There is also a fair amount of "drug-cocktail" use, as some students will drop a Xanax, Lithium or Vicodin (or even all three for that matter) into their drinks in order to enhance their night. Of course these people are the exception, not the rule. Cocaine has also seen a rise in popularity, which once again isn't surprising given the money that many students come from. Hallucinogens like mushroom and acid are also popular among the drug crowd, but as with all drugs at Lehigh, no one should ever feel forced or pressured to partake; drugs are around but you don't have to be around them.

The College Prowler™ Grade on
Drug Scene: B

A high grade in the Drug Scene indicates that drugs are not a noticeable part of campus life; drug use is not visible, and no pressure to use them seems to exist.

Campus Strictness

The Lowdown On...
Campus Strictness

What Are You Most Likely to Get Caught Doing on Campus?

- Fraternities holding unregistered parties (50 or more people in the house constitutes a party)
- Drinking underage
- Getting busted for drugs
- Driving drunk
- Public urination
- Parking illegally
- Having candles in your room

Students Speak Out On...
Campus Strictness

> "They can be quite strict at times, but tend to let us drink without much hassle. They don't tolerate drugs. I'll put it this way: I party a lot and I've never been given a problem with drinking in four years."

Q "The campus police, although **they have apparently been cracking down**, do allow us to have fun."

Q "The police try to seem stricter than they are. Though they break up a lot of parties on the Hill and now even off-campus, that does very little to stop the party – **everyone winds up relocating elsewhere**."

Q "I feel like the police are **way too strict**, but apparently they are much worse at most other schools, so I guess they aren't as bad as I thought."

Q "**They are VERY STRICT!** They are constantly busting parties and are not very friendly towards students."

Q "**The police are trying to crack down on drinking and drug use**, but if you're not stupid, it won't be a problem for you."

Q "**The police are a little too concerned** with drinking when they could be worrying about other important issues (muggings, rapes, etc.)."

Q "It's not that bad, although if you're underage you're dead! **Don't get caught drinking** underage or you'll lose your license for 90 days and spend the day in the judge's office, who then has to drive you home because you're probably a freshman and don't have a car!"

Q "The campus police are not particularly strict but the **Bethlehem police are.** Two of my close friends and I incurred drinking violations within our first semester at Lehigh. They have cracked down considerably in the last few years."

Q "**Campus police have been** extremely active in busting up fraternity parties this year. There's a whole range of theories as to why this is happening. I'll just say that apparently the Lehigh experience is nowhere near as crazy as it was 5 years ago. Despite this, you'll still have no problem finding a party to get to, and the police are never going to bother to arrest every underage kid at the parties they break up."

The College Prowler Take On...
Campus Strictness

Lehigh students often hear the age-old complaint from jaded alumni about how "the school isn't as fun as it was five years ago." For starters, kegs of any kind are completely banned from campus, so any fraternity caught with a keg will almost automatically be kicked out. Instead of kegs, every house buys cases upon cases of cheap beer, and this is more desirous anyway because it eliminates the ever-present lines inherent in having a party with a keg and makes the transition between games of Beirut much faster. All Lehigh parties are supposed to be registered, which entails having security guards present to ensure that no one underage is consuming alcohol. Usually the police won't make a big deal out of it if the house president is available and sober enough to have a reasonable conversation, but every now and then the police will enter a house and find the remnants of a great night of Beirut (flipped tables, beer-soaked floors, empty cans of Beast and plastic cups strewn about) and write the fraternity up. Depending on how strong the evidence is, the house can be put on social probation, and if they're already on probation may also face expulsion from the Hill.

In spite of these seemingly difficult restrictions, parties still continue to occur every weekend and beer is always readily available and in abundance. If you're a freshman drinking at a fraternity party and the cops come, you won't get in trouble as long as you're not blackout drunk. The other main illegal activities you may get caught doing are stumbling around campus drunk and underage, and selling or buying pot. A fair amount of freshman get written up for and some even go to the hospital for alcohol during the first few months of school because many kids come to college without any kind of notion as to what their limits are and wind up going all-out in such an unrestricted environment. Drug dealers are much more likely to get busted than purchasers, but if you leave drugs or drug paraphernalia out in your room during a fire alarm (and these happen very frequently), you may have some explaining to do. The police are doggedly persistent against narcotics, so it's a wise idea to stay away from drugs.

The College Prowler™ Grade on
Campus Strictness: C+

A high Campus Strictness grade implies an overall lenient atmosphere; police and RAs are fairly tolerant, and the administration's rules are flexible.

Parking

The Lowdown On...
Parking

Approximate Parking Permit Cost
$50 to park in your fraternity/sorority parking lot

Lehigh Parking Services
Scott, (610) 758-6352
smm4@lehigh.edu
http://www.lehigh.edu/~inpark/

Common Parking Tickets:
Expired Meter: $15, $35 after 3 offenses
No Parking Zone: $15, $35 after 3 offenses
Handicapped Zone: $50
Fire Lane: $50

Student Parking Lot?
Yes

Freshman Allowed to Park?
No, freshman aren't allowed to have cars

Parking Permits

There are parking permits available for all fraternity and sorority parking lots, as well as the parking lots for upperclass on-campus dorms. The permits are available on a first-come, first-serve basis.

Did You Know?

Best Places to Find a Parking Spot
Your best bet is on Packer Avenue, where many class buildings are located, or the Zoellner parking garage. If you try to park on campus between the hours of 7 a.m. – 4 p.m. expect to find a ticket on your windshield upon returning to your car.

Good Luck Getting a Parking Spot Here!
Anywhere on campus.

Students Speak Out On...
Parking

"**Don't get me started! Be prepared to pay out of your ass for parking on campus and in front of your own house or dormitory. There is NOT enough parking, and the little there is, is outrageous. Don't exceed time** limits because they'll be on you. And God forbid you park on campus before 4 p.m., it'll cost you about $35."

Q "Parking can be **quite annoying** on campus. There are legal spots for students (not freshman) but let's just say prepare for some tickets. Once you're in a fraternity it gets much easier and you don't get ticketed as much."

Q "**Nope, do not bring a car** freshman year. I don't think it's impossible to park though, if you know what time to leave for class it isn't that bad."

Q "**Parking is terrible!** Lehigh makes a fortune off my parking tickets alone."

Q "**Parking is really annoying** and I would say that there's no need to drive to class unless you live on the Hill in one of the higher houses. The meters take 25 cents for every half hour on lower campus, so it really adds up if you have a full day of class."

Q "You have to have a parking permit for the lots. **You can only park in your designated lot** and you get your stickers based on a first come first serve basis. It's moderately easy to park."

Q "**It sucks to park**. All the spots are reserved for faculty. They need to create more parking spots and stop giving out so many tickets."

Q "Parking on campus sucks - **it is beyond difficult to park**. It drives me crazy; Lehigh gives out parking tickets constantly."

Q "Parking is a bit of a game on campus. Tickets are handed out like candy, but no one pays them. **There is a limited number of spots**, and everyone drives. Most people just end up parking in the garages on campus."

Q "**Parking is horrible**. There are about 3000 BMWs and only four spots. Don't bother driving to class unless you can afford to pay $1,000 in parking tickets."

Q "The parking situation sucks, **I spent over $400 in parking tickets** my junior year alone."

Q "Parking on campus isn't easy, and sometimes particularly annoying. **Parking off-campus becomes much easier** with parking permits."

Q "**Honestly, parking sucks**. But you don't really need a car to get around. Everything is walking distance and I'm sure if you need to go somewhere, someone will be more than happy to take you."

Q "**Freshmen aren't permitted to have cars,** but if you are like me, then you're going to find a way to do it anyway. There's a secret street off campus (Meade St.) that freshman tend to park their cars on. They will not get ticketed there, but it tends to get crowded as more freshman find out."

The College Prowler Take On...
Parking

Parking on Lehigh's campus during an average weekday is nothing short of a disaster. Parking regulations are very strict. The only spots on campus are provided for faculty, which means if you try to park in these spots from 7 a.m. to 4 p.m. you are almost guaranteed to get ticketed. The only on-campus parking for students are a few 20-minute meter spots outside the upper University Center area. If you're even a second late returning to your car you will probably get a ticket. Most students will try their luck on Packer Avenue, which is the main thoroughfare at the bottom of campus. There are a number of free spots as well as metered spots, though it can get frustrating circling back and forth endlessly. The best time to look for a spot is right on the hour, as classes are getting out, because there is a significant amount of turnover. Students can also buy a parking pass for the Zoellner parking deck, which is very convenient for students in the business school.

This is all something of a moot point for freshmen, though. Freshmen aren't supposed to bring cars to school anyway, but clever-minded students can find parking off-campus is they're willing to look for it. The problem with off-campus parking is that you then run into the problem of dealing with the Bethlehem Parking Authority rather than the Lehigh Parking people, and the BPA can be just as persistent. Parking on campus does get easier after freshman year, once you join a fraternity or sorority you can obtain a parking permit for your house's lot, and all on campus dorms and apartments have parking lots as well. Parking is still a tremendous pain in the butt, as much of Lehigh's campus was built before cars even existed. As such, there are plenty of bizarre one-way roads, and driving around campus can be a confusing endeavor to the uninitiated. There have been talks of turning Lehigh into a completely pedestrian campus, but that's a very unlikely scenario, because then students wouldn't be able to showboat around campus in their Beemers anymore.

The College Prowler™ Grade on
Parking: D

A high grade in this section indicates that parking is both available and affordable, and that parking enforcement isn't overly severe.

Transportation

The Lowdown On...
Transportation

Ways to Get Around Town
On Campus
*Transportation Service*s
126 Goodman Drive
Bethlehem, PA 18015
Telephone: (610)758-4410
Fax: (610)758-5500

There is a free bus service available, operated by Transportation Services that runs from 7:40 a.m. – 10:10 p.m. and travels from main campus (Asa Packer) to both Goodman and Mountaintop campuses.

T.R.A.C.S.
(Take A Ride Around Campus Safely) van service runs 10 p.m. – 2:05 a.m. Sunday through Wednesday nights and 10 p.m. – 2:50 a.m. Thursday through Saturday nights.

Public Transportation
Bethlehem provides local bus transportation (LANTA Metro) to major parts of Bethlehem and nearby cities such as Hellertown and Allentown.
(610) 776-7433

Taxi Cabs

Lehigh Valley Taxi
(610) 867-5855

Car Rentals

Alamo, local: (610) 820-6907; national: (800) 327-9633
www.alamo.com

Avis, local: (610) 264-4450; national: (800) 831-2847
www.avis.com

Dollar, local: (610) 231-8785; national: (800) 800-4000
www.dollar.com

Enterprise, local: (610) 746-3300; national: (800) 736-8222,
www.enterprise.com

Best Ways to Get Around Town

Driving, walking

Ways to Get Out of Town

Airlines Serving Bethlehem
Continental, (800) 523-3273
www.continental.com
Delta, (800) 221-1212
www.delta-air.com
Northwest, (800) 225-2525
www.nwa.com
United, (800) 241-6522
www.united.com
US Airways, (800) 428-4322
www.usairways.com

Airport:

Lehigh Valley International Airport, (610) 266-6000
LVI is 10 miles and approximately 15 minutes driving time from Lehigh.

How to Get There:

Taxi

A Cab Ride to the Airport Costs:

$20

Trans-Bridge Lines

The Trans-Bridge Bus Terminal is on the South Side of Bethlehem, approximately 1 mile from campus. For schedule information, call (610) 868-6001.
www.transbridge.com

Trans-Bridge Bus Terminal

Adams Street & Mechanic Street
Bethlehem, PA 18015
(610) 868-6001

Travel Agents

Designing vacations by Sandi
217 9th Ave., Allentown
(610) 419-1352

Students Speak Out On...
Transportation

> "Public transportation is not really convenient at all. I never took it and neither did many other people I knew. The Lehigh bus system brings you around campus and into the beginning of town and that is very easy to use."

Q "**Is there public transportation**? Mostly everything you need is on campus."

Q "**It's not convenient** but everything is within walking distance and after freshman year **everyone has a car.**"

Q "**It's not very convenient**. However, most students have cars so it is not a problem. There should be more transportation at night."

Q "**T.R.A.C.S**. is a great thing for the students at Lehigh. It takes you anywhere and is a safe alternative to hoping in a car with a drunk driver. Also the buses that drive around campus during the day are helpful during the winter months."

Q "**Do we even have public transportation?** I can honestly say that you will catch about five of the 4500 undergrads at Lehigh on LANTA. Just say no."

Q "**Is this a joke?** There is nothing 'in town' worth seeing. You really don't leave campus except to go to the bar, and even then it's practically across the street."

Q "There really isn't any that I know of and you really don't need any. **Almost everywhere you'd hang out at Lehigh is within walking distance**."

Q "**Public transportation is not very available**. Getting around is much easier after freshman year if a student can bring a car, though that's not to say that freshman year without a car is miserable. It is much better to not have a car; stick around campus and have the true freshman experience.'"

Q "**Not too many taxis around**, but there is a shuttle to the mall. There is a bus station in town, and an airport nearby. The campus provides transportation by bus during the day and van at night. You can get around pretty good."

Q "**Lehigh runs its own service late-nights** on the weekends that runs from off-campus to the top of the "Hill" (where most of the fraternities are). You'll never need to worry about getting to a party when it's raining. As far as out-of-town transportation, there's a bus station a few blocks off-campus that runs to both Philly and NYC, among other places. There isn't much that takes you around Bethlehem though."

The College Prowler Take On...
Transportation

Public transportation is essentially nonexistent in Bethlehem. Sure, there's a public bus, but no one from Lehigh's ever been on it. The town is small enough that as a freshman you can walk just about anywhere you'd need to get to, and chances are you'll meet someone who does have a car anyway. Lehigh provides a bus service around campus as well as the all-important T.R.A.C.S. van for drunken traveling at night. There is also a shuttle to the Lehigh Valley Mall on weekends, which is highly recommended just as a means of getting away from campus for a bit.

There is also a bus station right in town which can take you to New York City or Pennsylvania and the Lehigh Valley International airport is a 15-minute ride away from campus. Cab service is poor at best, and good luck trying to get a cab at 2 a.m. after a long night at the bar in an attempt to get back on the Hill. Most students would agree that the best way to get anywhere is by car, be it class, restaurants, Allentown, or NYC. Having a car after freshman year is crucial, especially on Lehigh's hilly campus. The freedom you have is unparalleled and as fun as freshman year can be, it only gets better once you have a car.

The College Prowler™ Grade on
Transportation: C

A high grade for Transportation indicates that campus buses, public buses, cabs, and rental cars are readily-available and affordable. Other determining factors include proximity to an airport and the necessity of transportation.

Weather

The Lowdown On...
Weather

Average Temperature
Fall: 52 °F
Winter: 30 °F
Spring: 50 °F
Summer: 71 °F

Average Precipitation
Fall: 3.8 in.
Winter: 3.21 in.
Spring: 3.84 in.
Summer: 4.2 in.

Students Speak Out On...
Weather

> "It gets really cold and snowy in the winter here, and given the size of the hills, I'd wrap up. Once the weather does break, it is a continuous outdoor party until students get out for summer break."

- "**Bring summer and fall clothing** until thanksgiving break, then bring winter clothing. It's always hot in the dorms, and you will always wear a tank top out."

- "**The weather is the same as the northeast**. Sweaters in the winter, tank tops in the summer."

- "**Pretty much like the rest of the northeast**. The nicest times are the early fall and then in spring people walk around campus in sweatshirts, jeans, flip-flops - very laid back."

- "The **weather ranges everywhere from 20 degrees and snowy to 100 degrees and humid**. I would bring it all."

- "It fluctuates. **Bring sweaters and t-shirts,** jeans and shorts, also nicer stuff to go out in. Sweatpants are also key for class."

- "**It is typical east coast weather**. It's nice in the spring, cold in the winter. Bring clothes for all four seasons."

- "We're in rural Pennsylvania. **It's cold in the winter**."

Q "**Moderate** is what they call it, but bring every type of clothing you have. Lord only knows how hot or cold it could get in any given year."

Q "When it's the **spring and fall the weather is beautiful!** When it's sunny and warm at Lehigh we have awesome BBQs! What's better in life than playing Beirut and eating a cheeseburger at the same time? Life doesn't get better than that, especially when it's nice out. Go shopping at the Salvation Army for clothes."

Q "**Spring and fall are pretty nice**, summer is hot and humid and winter is pretty cool but pretty snowy, usually enough to close the school at least once a year."

Q "**It's seasonal** - we have 90 degree days where we hang out outside all day and We've had snowstorms with 3 feet of snow. Bring everything you own."

The College Prowler Take On...
Weather

Expect typical northeast weather in Bethlehem. As students return to school in late August, there should still be about a month of reasonably warm shorts weather. The beginning of October usually sees cooler weather, and by November it starts getting much colder. Bethlehem winters are pretty unforgiving. Even if it's not snowing, it's very cold, and when it does snow, it snows a ton. The snow makes getting around very inconvenient, especially since Lehigh is situated on a hill. The cold weather also sees a noticeable mood change in most students. Even though everyone parties year round, the winter can make Lehigh seem very bleak, but around March sprits begin to lift again with the advent of warmer weather.

Once the warm weather comes in, the last month or so of school is one non-stop party. Pledging is over and fraternities have barbeques almost every day. You can't drive around the Hill without seeing at least 10 guys per house hanging outside in their parking lot. It's an incredibly relaxed atmosphere, and is one of the greatest aspects of being at Lehigh. The warm weather lifts everyone's moods; and the only downside is that the end of the year is near and those great, carefree times can't last forever.

The College Prowler™ Grade on
Weather: C+

A high Weather grade designates that temperatures are mild and rarely reach extremes, that the campus tends to be sunny rather than rainy, and that weather is fairly consistent rather than unpredictable.

LEHIGH UNIVERSITY
Report Card Summary

B+ ACADEMICS	**B+** GUYS
C LOCAL ATMOSPHERE	**B+** GIRLS
A- SAFETY AND SECURITY	**B+** ATHLETICS
B+ COMPUTERS	**C+** NIGHTLIFE
B+ FACILITIES	**A+** GREEK LIFE
B CAMPUS DINING	**B** DRUG SCENE
B+ OFF-CAMPUS DINING	**C+** CAMPUS STRICTNESS
B+ CAMPUS HOUSING	**D** PARKING
B OFF-CAMPUS HOUSING	**C** TRANSPORTATION
D+ DIVERSITY	**C+** WEATHER

Overall Experience

Students Speak Out On...
Overall Experience

"I loved Lehigh and all it had to offer me. People always talk about how great it used to be, but I had a crazy four years that I wouldn't trade for anything. My only complaint would be the size of the student body. If I change anything, I'd bring some more people there because after awhile everyone knows your business, and you need to find girls in the weirdest places."

Q "**I love Lehigh**! I'm having the best time and wouldn't want to change a thing!"

Q "**Best school ever**. Join the Greek system and you're guaranteed to make the most of college. I wouldn't have wanted to go anywhere else."

Q "The **only thing that makes Lehigh so great is the party scene** and the friends I've made here. Other than that I wouldn't recommend it to anyone else."

Q "**I love school**; I would never have gone anywhere else. While adjusting to college was an interesting and challenging experience, I could not be more pleased with my life at Lehigh. I have good professors, a good circle of close friends, and a good social life. And, most importantly, I'm happy."

Q "**Lehigh has been great for me.** I have made the best of friends and have been given the opportunity to grow academically and as a person. I truly love Lehigh and would not be happier anywhere else."

Q "**I've loved every minute here at Lehigh**. I couldn't imagine myself anywhere else. It's a perfect school for me and I couldn't be happier."

Q "**I love Lehigh**! When I was deciding on where to go to school, I had so many choices, but I was unsure as to where I would be truly happy. I now know that Lehigh was the right place for me!"

Q "Only place I can imagine spending my college years. It had the perfect elements - **a beautiful green campus**, a fun social scene, a good reputation, and only about an hour away from NYC and Philly."

Q "**It was an amazing experience** and I wish I could go back."

Q "I wish I went to school in Los Angeles or **someplace a bit more exciting than Bethlehem**."

Q "I wouldn't have traded my experience at Lehigh for the world! I met some of the best friends I have ever had. I did things I could have never imagined possible. And, I partied harder than ever in what turned out to be the longest vacation of my life! **Lehigh was the best time of my life**, but I'm glad it's over."

Q "If I had to do it all over again, I wouldn't change a thing. **Lehigh all the way**! You bet my kids are going there."

Q "**I've had a positive experience**, although sometimes I wish I went to a school where 90% of the people weren't all about Prada bags, BMWs, Tiffany's, Audis, snooty and whiny. Basically Lehigh is not the place to find 'cool, normal or hot' girls."

Q "**Lehigh was, in a word, perfect.** I spent the best four years of my life there and I wouldn't trade it for the world."

Q "The overall experience at Lehigh is **a true college experience.** It is a great time inside and out. I would have never wanted to go somewhere else. The only aspect I questioned was missing out on 'city life,' but after spending a semester at a city school, I could not have appreciated Lehigh anymore."

Q "**There's something about this school that you just can't put into words**. Walking to class in the winter with the town of Bethlehem opening up underneath you, trudging up a steep hill at four in the morning with a Natty Ice in your hand, or just watching TV with your best friends in the frat house - I wouldn't change anything about my last four years. I can't imagine what would have happened to me if I hadn't gone to Lehigh. It was the best decision I ever made."

The College Prowler Take On...
Overall Experience

There's nothing quite like being an undergraduate at Lehigh University. There's a reason why many people call college "the best four years of your life," and that statement applies to Lehigh perfectly. While it may not be in the greatest town in the world, the winters can be harsh and the student body is incredibly homogenous, Lehigh students love their school. The professors are mostly knowledgeable and friendly, and academics play a huge role in any college student's experience, but the friendships forged and the outstanding social life are what make Lehigh students fall head over heels for their school. Freshmen enter Lehigh unsure of what awaits them, and emerge four years later wishing there was a way they could stay for another four years. You're thrown together in various dorms in hopes that you'll be able to coexist with each other, and for the first time in your life you have unlimited freedom; you take classes you hate and eat horrible meals in the dining halls, but the Hill still has an intriguing, almost otherworldly aura about it.

From freshman through senior year, each has its own distinctive memories, and the entire four-year duration can almost feel like a dream at times. Many have called their time at Lehigh a fantasy, and there are few other experiences in life where that statement will be applicable.

The Inside Scoop

The Lowdown On...
The Inside Scoop

Lehigh Slang

Know the slang, know the school. The following is a list of things you really need to know before coming to Lehigh. The more of these words you know, the better off you'll be.

The Hill: The area situated above the main campus where all of the fraternity houses are located as well as a few sorority houses. The Hill is the main social hub at Lehigh until senior year. Many students will wind up spending more time on the Hill than anywhere else on campus, classes and the library included.

M & M: McClintic & Marshall freshman dorm

Lower Cents: Centennial II freshman dorm

The U.C.: The University Center

Beirut Leg: Usually obtained by leaners, Beirut leg is a large beer stain on the front of your pants.

Leaning: Leaners are thought to have an unfair advantage in Beirut, but it's perfectly legal and may be advantageous to longer-limbed players

Four-Cup: A very rare shot in Beirut in which there are only four cups remaining, and the ball actually lands and remains in the center of the four-cup square, ending the game

Hotels: A popular fraternity party in which each brother's room contains a different mixed drink

100-Cup: A 100-cup version of Beirut created at Lehigh. Each team is comprised of four players. Play requires a case of beer as well as 100 cups per side. There is no re-racking; you merely place the empty cup right back where you picked it up, and the first team to clear all 100 cups wins, as long as the other team fails to hit their rebuttal shots. It's a Lehigh hallmark that many have attempted, but few can play without throwing up at least once during the course of the game.

The Bone: Rathbone Dining Hall

T.R.A.C.S.: The free nightly van service around campus

The Brown and White: Lehigh's official school newspaper; also the school's official colors

Gryphon: Residence Hall Advisor

Fairmart: Fairchild-Martindale Library

The Goose: Goosey Gander deli, a student favorite. Also fraternities tend to have a member nicknamed The Goose as well.

Registered party: Every party at Lehigh is supposed to be registered, which means security guards must be present and you need to be 21 in order to get a wristband which enables you to drink. Registered parties are usually held every weekend, and can range from dance parties to cocktails.

Unregistered party: These go on almost every night of the week. Lehigh considers an unregistered party any event in which more than 50 people are present and there is alcohol being consumed. And yet more Beirut is played on a daily basis than any other activity at Lehigh. Go figure.

Brownies: Lehigh's version of rent-a-cop. The Brownies, decked in all brown, patrol the Hill at night in search of unregistered parties. If they do indeed find one, they notify the Lehigh University police to break up the party.

Mardi Gras: The biggest party of the year, generally held in April by Delta Phi fraternity, this indoor/outdoor party is always the wildest and drunkest party students will attend all year.

Things I Wish I Knew Before Coming to Lehigh

- Greek life completely dominates the social scene.
- It's a huge party school.
- The journalism department is highly underrated.
- Engineering is the hardest major.
- You're most likely to get a job right away through the business school.
- The town of Bethlehem has a lot more hidden treasures than most people realize.
- Though Lehigh's been attempting to balance things out, it's still a far better school for business and engineering than arts & sciences.
- You can skip most big lecture classes and still do well as long as you read the textbook.

Tips to Succeed at Lehigh

- Join a fraternity/sorority.
- Network with your house's alumni.
- Give yourself ample time to study for exams.
- Go to your major classes.
- Have an idea of what you want to major in before coming to Lehigh.
- Pick classes you think you will enjoy.
- Stay away from 7:55 classes.

Lehigh Urban Legends

- In 1998, Jennifer Love Hewitt was rumored to be attending Lehigh as a freshman.
- Playboy ranked Lehigh the #1 party school in the country at some point in the 90s.
- The administration wants to get rid of every last fraternity.

School Spirit

Lehigh's school spirit comes out at random occasions, but on the whole you'd find most students to be fairly apathetic about school spirit in general. School spirit is at its highest right before home football games, as everyone comes together in drunken revelry at tailgates. As euphoric an experience as tailgates is, it's also quite exhausting, and many students leave before the football game even starts. The only other sport with a decent amount of school spirit is wrestling, a sport that is huge in Pennsylvania and one that Lehigh has always had a nice amount of success with. As much as many students enjoy their time at Lehigh immensely, a good portion of them don't feel a true sense of school pride until after they have graduated.

Traditions

Tailgates

Tailgates are an incredibly popular long-standing tradition. When Lehigh has a home football game on Saturday, many students wake up at 8 a.m. to start drinking. Fraternities have morning cocktails, followed by the actual tailgating near the football field. Tailgates is the only event at Lehigh where students don't have to worry about being caught drinking. Beer, barbeques and fun in the sun – it doesn't get much better.

Lehigh-Lafayette football game

The oldest rivalry in college sports, the Lehigh-Lafayette football game is a true classic. This weekend sees more alumni return than any other weekend throughout the entire year. Fraternities and sororities plan weekend-long events capped off by huge dinners on Saturday night. It's a great weekend to catch up with old friends and classmates and enjoy watching Lehigh annihilate Lafayette.

Greek Week

Every year in April, the newly initiated members from all the fraternities and sororities participate in Greek Week, filled with competitions ranging from hot-dog eating, to dancing, to a bachelor auction, to Mr. Lehigh and Dream Girl contests. The house with the most points wins Greek Week. On top of the events, Greek Week is often cited as the most enjoyable week of the year, as fraternities have parties and barbeques scheduled all day and all night for the entire week. For many students, it will be the drunkest week of their lives.

Fraternity rush

The time during which freshman interested in going Greek must decide which house is the best fit for them. Rush events include dinners at the house, dinners at restaurants, Beirut tournaments and trips to New York City. By the end of rush, freshmen should have an excellent idea of where to pledge.

Sorority rush

Sorority rush is much different than fraternity rush, as it lasts only two weeks and takes place at the beginning of spring semester. In this brief two-week period, freshmen girls are supposed to decided which house will be the best fit for them for the next four years. Surprisingly, most girls wind up being happy with the decisions they make.

Important area stores

Lighthouse Washbasket and Dry Cleaner
Wash and Fold service, Laundromat and Dry Cleaning
1621 Stefko Blvd., Bethlehem
(610) 867-7755

American Hairlines
Hair Salon
38 W. Broad St., Historic Bethlehem
(610) 882-9848

CVS
Pharmacy and convenience store
305 W. 4th Street, South Side Bethlehem
(610) 691-4085

Cantelmi's Ace Hardware
Hardware
521-529 E. 4th Street, South Side Bethlehem
(610) 691-2995

Lehigh Valley Mall
Route 22 and Route 145N, MacArthur Road, Whitehall
(610) 264-5511

Best Buy
1504 MacArthur Road, Whitehall
(610) 432-6956

Saucon Square
Shopping Center, rte. 378

Super Fresh
Supermarket
(610) 691-5011

Saucon Square Dry Cleaners
Dry cleaning
(610) 317-6464

Blockbuster Video
Movie rentals
(610) 865-5996

Radio Shack
Electronics
(610) 694-0387

Finding a Job or Internship

The Lowdown On...
Finding a Job or Internship

According to Career Services, the average Lehigh graduate salary is $41,460.

They do not categorize by major.

Finding a job after graduating can be difficult, but Lehigh's Career Services office is here to help. On top of Career Services, students will also find networking opportunities at Lehigh's numerous Career Fairs, where many top companies recruit heavily.

Advice

Stay in regular contact with Career Services, as they will do their best to guide you in the right direction. Make sure you attend at least one Career Fair. For those students in Greek organizations, your alumni can be a huge advantage when it comes to networking and finding a job. Always keep all possible avenues open; you never know who you'll meet that may lead you to that elusive first job.

Career Center Resources & Services

- Office of Career Services

- LUCIE – Lehigh University Career Information exchange

Career Services' web site: www.career.lehigh.edu

Percent of Grads who Enter Job Market Within 6 Months After Graduation:
57%

Firms That Most Frequently Hire Graduates:
Accenture; KPMG; PricewaterhouseCoopers; Ernst & Young; Deloitte & Touche; Northrop Grumman; Merrill Lynch; Ingersoll-Rand; MBNA America Bank; US Army; Johnson & Johnson; Lockheed Martin; UBS PaineWebber; Black & Decker; Rothstein, Kass & Co. SEI Investments; Standard & Poor's; Sunoco; Merck; Air Products & Chemicals; IBM; AT&T; JP Morgan Chase; Enterprise Rent-A-Car; Lehigh University; Pfizer, Inc. American Express; Aventis Pasteur; Cintas Corp. Sure Fit, Inc. The Trane Company; The Vanguard Group; APP Technologies; Automatic Data Processing, Inc. Bank One Card Services; Clark Construction Group; Computer Aid, Inc. Grant Thornton; Kiewit Construction Co. Macy's; Media Edge; National Institute of Health; Raytheon Co. Robert Stern Associates; Torcon; Wyeth Pharmaceuticals

The Lowdown On...
Alumni

Website:
www3.lehigh.edu/alumni/

Office:
Alumni Association
Lehigh University
27 Memorial Drive West
Bethlehem, PA 18015
(610) 758-3135

Services Available
Lifetime e-mail address

The Alumni Association:

The Alumni Association is located in the admissions building. It is open during normal business hours. The mission statement of the Association is "To maintain and cultivate among its members a sentiment of regard for one another and affection and attachment to Lehigh University and to support and promote in every way the interests of Lehigh University."

Major Alumni Events

There is a Young Alumni weekend that takes place during the second weekend of October, in which alumni from recent years participate in class gatherings, dinners and a networking reception. Of course, the main alumni event is Lehigh-Lafayette weekend (see words to know).

Alumni Publications

Lehigh Alumni Bulletin

Produced for the Alumni Association on a quarterly basis, the Alumni Bulletin is an attractive, full-color editorial magazine that is provided free as a service to Lehigh alumni, friends and parents of current students.

Did You Know?

Famous Lehigh Alumni:

Lee Iacocca

Donny Most

Tucker Quayle

Robert Durst

Student Organizations

There are more than 400 student organizations on campus. The following is a partial list:

Accounting Club – www.lehigh.edu/~inactcl/index.html

Alpha Phi Omega Service Fraternity – www.lehigh.edu/~inapo.html

Amaranth - Lehigh's Literary Magazine – www.lehigh.edu/~inamr/index.html

American Institute of Chemical Engineers (AIChE)-- Student Chapter – www.lehigh.edu/~inice

American Society of Civil Engineers - Student Chapter – www.lehigh.edu/~inasce

Asian Cultural Society – www.lehigh.edu/~inasian

Association for Computing Machinery Student Group – acm.cse.lehigh.edu

Best Buddies Club – www.lehigh.edu/~inbuddi/

Cheerleading Club – www.lehigh.edu/~incheer/

Chinese Students & Scholars Association – www.lehigh.edu/~incsa/incsa.html

Lehigh Crew – www.lehigh.edu/~incrw/

Drown Writer's Series – www.lehigh.edu/~indws/

Epitome (Yearbook) – www.lehigh.edu/~inyear/

Equestrian Club – www.lehigh.edu/~inequest/

Fellowship of Christian Athletes – www.lehigh.edu/~infca/

Lehigh University Fencing Club – www.lehigh.edu/~infence/

FONI Club – www.lehigh.edu/~infoni/

Frisbee Club – www.lehigh.edu/~inuft/inuft.html

Future Global Entrepreneur Club – www.lehigh.edu/~infge/fge.html

Gaming Club – www.lehigh.edu/~ingam/

GLASS – www.lehigh.edu/~inglass/inglass.html

Graduate Student Council – www.lehigh.edu/~ingsc/ingsc.html

Ice Hockey Team – www.lehigh.edu/~inhky/

Ice Hockey Team "B" – www.lehigh.edu/~inhkyb/inhkyb.html

Indian Students Association – www.lehigh.edu/~inisa/

Institute of Electrical and Electronics Engineers (IEEE) Student Branch – www.lehigh.edu/~inieee/

Kappa Kappa Psi – www.lehigh.edu/~inkkp/

Korean Student Club – www.lehigh.edu/~inksc/indextop.html

Lehigh Christian Fellowship – www.lehigh.edu/~inlcf/

Lehigh for Life – www.lehigh.edu/~inlulife

Lehigh University Emergency Medical Services – www.lehigh.edu/~inluems/

Marching '97 – www.lehigh.edu/~inbnd/

MBA Association – www.lehigh.edu/~inmba/

Mustard & Cheese Drama Society – www.lehigh.edu/~inmac/

Newman Council – www.lehigh.edu/~innew/

Odyssey of the Mind Club – www.lehigh.edu/~inluodsy/

Outing Club – www.lehigh.edu/~inotg/

Public Relations Student Society Of America – www.lehigh.edu/~inprssa/

Reformed University Fellowship – www.lehigh.edu/~inruf

Russian Club – www.lehigh.edu/~inruscl

Safespace: Gay/Lesbian/Bisexual Ally program – www.lehigh.edu/~safspace/

Ski Team – www.lehigh.edu/~inski/

Society of Automotive Engineers – www.lehigh.edu/~insae/

Society of Hispanic Professional Engineers – www.lehigh.edu/~inshpe/

Society of Manufacturing Engineers – www.lehigh.edu/~insme/

Student Materials Society – www.lehigh.edu/~inmrc/inmrc.html

Swing Club – www.lehigh.edu/~inswing/

Lehigh University Table-Tennis (Ping-Pong) Club – www.lehigh.edu/~inping/

Tau Beta Pi Engineering Honor Society – www.lehigh.edu/~intbp/

Taiwanese Student Club – www.lehigh.edu/~inchiclb

Turkish Students Association – www.lehigh.edu/~intsa/

Turkish Students Club – www.lehigh.edu/~inturkey/

Volleyball (Men's) Club – www.lehigh.edu/~involley/

WLVR Radio Station – www.lehigh.edu/~inwlvr/

The Best & The Worst

The Ten **BEST** Things About Lehigh:

1. Greek Life
2. Playing Beirut
3. The Wonderful Student Body
4. Fraternity Parties
5. Tailgates
6. Sociable Students
7. Proximity to New York City
8. Greek Week
9. Lehigh-Lafayette Weekend
10. Fraternity Date Parties, Sorority Formals

The Ten **WORST** Things About Lehigh:

1. Parties Frequently Getting Busted by Cops
2. Mounting Parking Tickets
3. Harsh Bethlehem Winters
4. Bethlehem....
5. Drunken Hook-ups
6. The Upper UC Food Court
7. Four o' Clocks & Finals
8. The Greek Scene Can Get Repetitive
9. Having to Balance Work & Play
10. It Only Lasts Four Years!

Visiting LU

The Lowdown On...
Visiting LU

Hotel Information

Radisson Hotel Bethlehem
www.radisson.com
437 Main Street
Bethlehem, PA 18018
(610) 625-5000
Distance from campus: less than a mile
Price range: $140-$225

Comfort Inn Bethlehem
www.comfortbethlehem.com
US 22 and Rte. 191
Bethlehem, PA 18020
(610) 865-6300
Distance from campus: 1 mile
Price range: $89-$105

Comfort Suites University
www.comfortsuitesbethlehem.com
120 W. 3rd Street
Bethlehem, PA 18015
(610) 882-9700
Distance from campus: less than a mile
Price range: $85-$120

Courtyard Bethlehem
www.courtyard.com
2160 Motel Drive
Bethlehem, PA 18018
(610) 317-6200
Distance from campus: 2 miles
Price range: $119-$155

Fairfield Inn Bethlehem

Courtyard Bethlehem (Cont...)
Distance from campus: 2 miles
Price range: $119-$155

Fairfield Inn Bethlehem
www.fairfieldinn.com
2140 Motel Drive
Bethlehem, PA 18018
(610) 867-8681
Distance from campus: 2 miles
Price range: $115-$160

Holiday Inn Bethlehem
www.ichotelsgroup.com
Route 512 and Route 22
Bethlehem, PA 18017
(610) 866-5800
Distance from campus: 5 miles
Price range: $105-$170

Residence Inn Allentown
www.marriot.com
2180 Motel Drive
Bethlehem, PA 18018
(610) 317-2662
Distance from campus: 2 miles
Price range: $119-$175

Take a Campus Virtual Tour
www3.lehigh.edu/about/vtours/entertours.html

To Schedule a Group Information Session or Interview
Call the Office of Admissions at (610) 758-3100 to schedule an appointment or interview. Group Information Sessions are offered Monday through Friday at 9 a.m., 10 a.m. and 11 a.m. Advanced reservations are not required.

Campus Tours
Campus tours are given Monday through Friday at 10:15 a.m., 11:15 a.m., 1:00 p.m. and 3:15 p.m. Advanced reservations are not required.

Overnight Visits
High school seniors may spend the day as a Lehigh student. Visits may include sitting in on classes, having a meal at one of our on-campus eateries, spending time in a dorm room, participation in campus events and spending time with undergraduate students. The Day in the Life program begins in Admissions at 8:45 a.m. and includes an afternoon campus tour and a group information session. The program concludes by 3:15 p.m.

Directions to Campus

From Route 22:

For those who must use Route 22, take Route 378 exit in Bethlehem. Route 378 heads only south; continue for 3.6 miles and when you cross the bridge over the Lehigh River, being careful to stay in the left-turn lane, marked "Third Street." Bear left at the traffic light for Third Street at the south end of the bridge; continue one block to the traffic light at Brodhead Avenue, and turn right. At a four-way stop, continue through the Packer Avenue intersection. You will see the Alumni Memorial Building on your left. Turn left on to Memorial Drive West just below the Alumni Memorial Building, and make an immediate right into the visitors' parking lot in front of the building. This building, easily identified by its high stone tower, houses the Admissions Office on the first floor.

From Philadelphia and Southern New Jersey:

Take the Northeast Extension (Route 476) of the Pennsylvania Turnpike north to exit 44 (Quakertown). Turn left onto Route 663. Follow for 3.5 miles. Turn left onto Route 309 in Quakertown. Continue north on Route 309 to Center Valley. Turn right onto Route 378 north towards Bethlehem. Follow Route 378 over South Mountain. About halfway down the far side of the mountain, at the second set of yellow blinking lights, turn right onto Summit Street. At the end of Summit Street, the Alumni Memorial Building will be directly in front of you. There is a visitors' parking lot directly in front of the building.

From Route I-78 East or West:
From Route I-78:
Take the Hellertown/Bethlehem exit 67 (formerly 21).

From the east: Go straight at the end of the exit ramp across Route 412 onto Silvex Road (between Wendy's and Turkey Hill).

From the west: Turn right at the end of the exit ramp onto Route 412 North (Main Street). Turn left at the traffic light at Silvex Road. Continue on Silvex under the railroad overpass and across the creek. Saucon Park will be on your right. Go straight under I-78 and continue to William Street (you will see a sign for the Asa Packer Campus). At the stop sign go straight across William Street to College Drive. The athletic facilities of Lehigh's Murray Goodman Campus will be on your left. Turn right at the stop sign on Mountain Drive South and continue back under I-78 and through the next stop sign. Follow the Lehigh University directional signs for the Asa Packer Campus. Bear left at the fork at the top of the mountain. The entrance to Lehigh's Mountaintop Campus will be on your right. Continue on Mountain Drive through the first stop sign. Stay right at the fork past Lehigh's Sayre Fields and continue through the stop sign. Take the first left through the stone gates onto Upper Sayre Park Road. Follow Upper Sayre Park Road down the mountain. Turn left at the stop sign facing Taylor College (the tan residence). About 50 feet ahead is the next stop sign. Turn left onto University Drive and bear right where the road circles around Trembley Park Apartments. At the stop sign, turn left. At the next stop sign, turn left onto Memorial Drive West. The Alumni Memorial Building will be on your left, with the parking lot immediately past the building. The 4.5-mile drive should take approximately 10 minutes from the I-78 exit.

Words to Know

Academic Probation – A student can receive this if they fail to keep up with their school's academic minimums. Those who are unable to improve their grades after receiving this warning can possibly face dismissal.

Beer Pong / Beirut – A drinking game with numerous cups of beer arranged in a particular pattern on each side of a table. The goal is to get a ping pong ball into one of the opponent's cups by throwing the ball or hitting it with a paddle. If the ball lands in a cup, the opponent is required to drink the beer.

Bid – An invitation from a fraternity or sorority to pledge their specific house.

Blue-Light Phone – Brightly-colored phone posts with a blue light bulb on top. These phones exist for security purposes and are located at various outside locations around most campuses. If a student has an emergency or is feeling endangered, they can pick up one of these phones (free of charge) to connect with campus police or an escort service.

Campus Police – Policemen who are specifically assigned to a given institution. Campus police are not regular city officers; they are employed by the university in a full-time capacity.

Club Sports – A level of sports that falls somewhere between varsity and intramural. If a student is unable to commit to a varsity team but has a lot of passion for athletics, a club sport could be a better, less intense option. If a club sport still requires too much commitment, intramurals often involve no traveling and a lot less time.

Cocaine – An illegal drug. Also known as "coke" or "blow," cocaine often resembles a white crystalline or powdery substance. It is highly addictive and dangerous.

Common Application – An application that students can use to apply to multiple schools.

Course Registration – The time when a student selects what courses they would like for the upcoming quarter or semester. Prior to registration, it is best to have an idea of several back-up courses in case a particular class becomes full. If a course is full, a student can place themselves on the waitlist, although this still does not guarantee entry.

Division Athletics – Athletics range from Division I to Division III. Division IA is the most competitive, while Division III is considered to be the least competitive.

Dorm – Short for dormitory, a dorm is an on-campus housing facility. Dorms can provide a range of options from suite-style rooms to more communal options that include shared bathrooms. Most first-year students live in dorms. Some upperclassmen who wish to stay on campus also choose this option.

Early Action – A way to apply to a school and get an early acceptance response without a binding commitment. This is a system that is becoming less and less available.

Early Decision – An option that students should use only if they are positive that a place is their dream school. If a student applies to a school using the early decision option and is admitted, they are required and bound to attend that university. Admission rates are usually higher with early decision students because the school knows that a student is making them their first choice.

Ecstasy – An illegal drug. Also known as "E" or "X," ecstasy looks like a pill and most resembles an aspirin. Considered a party drug, ecstasy is very dangerous and can be deadly.

Ethernet – An extremely fast internet connection that is usually available in most university-owned residence halls. To use an Ethernet connection properly, a student will need a network card and cable for their computer.

Fake ID – A counterfeit identification card that contains false information. Most commonly, students get fake IDs and change their birthdates so that they appear to be older than 21 (of legal drinking age). Even though it is illegal, many college students have fake IDs in hopes of purchasing alcohol or getting into bars.

Frosh – Slang for "freshmen."

Hazing – Initiation rituals that must be completed for membership into some fraternities or sororities. Numerous universities have outlawed hazing due to its degrading or dangerous requirements.

Sports (IMs) – A popular, and usually free, student activity where students create teams and compete against other groups for fun. These sports vary in competitiveness and can include a range of activities—everything from billiards to water polo. IM sports are a great way to meet people with similar interests.

Keg – Officially called a half barrel, a keg contains roughly 200 12-ounce servings of beer and is often found at college parties.

LSD – An illegal drug. Also known as acid, this hallucinogenic drug most commonly resembles a tab of paper.

Marijuana – An illegal drug. Also known as weed or pot; besides alcohol, marijuana is one of the most commonly-found drugs on campuses across the country.

Major –The focal point of a student's college studies; a specific topic that is studied for a degree. Examples of majors include physics, English, history, computer science, economics, business, and music. Many students decide on a specific major before arriving on campus, while others are simply "undecided" and figure it out later. Those who are extremely interested in two areas can also choose to double major.

Meal Block – The equivalent of one meal. Students on a "meal plan" usually receive a fixed number of meals per week.

Each meal, or "block," can be redeemed at the school's dining facilities in place of cash. More often than not, if a student fails to use their weekly allotment of meal blocks, they will be forfeited.

Minor – An additional focal point in a student's education. Often serving as a compliment or addition to a student's main area of focus, a minor has fewer requirements and prerequisites to fulfill than a major. Minors are not required for graduation from most schools; however some students who want to further explore many different interests choose to have both a major and a minor.

Mushrooms – An illegal drug. Also known as "shrooms," this drug looks like regular mushrooms but are extremely hallucinogenic.

Off-Campus Housing – Housing from a particular landlord or rental group that is not affiliated with the university. Depending on the college, off-campus housing can range from extremely popular to non-existent. Those students who choose to live off campus are typically given more freedom, but they also have to deal with things such as possible subletting scenarios, furniture, and bills. In addition to these factors, rental prices and distance often affect a student's decision to move off campus.

Office Hours – Time that teachers set aside for students who have questions about the coursework. Office hours are a good place for students to go over any problems and to show interest in the subject material.

Pledging – The time after a student has gone through rush, received a bid, and has chosen a particular fraternity or sorority they would like to join. Pledging usually lasts anywhere from one to two semesters. Once the pledging period is complete and a particular student has done everything that is required to become a member, they are considered a brother or sister. If a fraternity or a sorority would decide to "haze" a group of students, these initiation rituals would take place during the pledging period.

Private Institution – A school that does not use taxpayers dollars to help subsidize education costs. Private schools typically cost more than public schools and are usually smaller.

Prof – Slang for "professor."

Public Institution – A school that uses taxpayers dollars to help subsidize education costs. Public schools are often a good value for in-state residents and tend to be larger than most private colleges.

Quarter System (sometimes referred to as the Trimester System) – A type of academic calendar system. In this setup, students take classes for three academic periods. The first quarter usually starts in late September or early October and concludes right before Christmas. The second quarter usually starts around early to mid–January and finishes up around March or April. The last quarter, or "third quarter," usually starts in late March or early April and finishes up in late May or Mid-June. The fourth quarter is summer. The major difference between the quarter system and semester system is that students take more courses but with less coverage.

RA (Resident Assistant) – A student leader who is assigned to a particular floor in a dormitory in order to help to the other students who live there. A RA's duties include ensuring student safety and providing guidance or assistance wherever possible.

Recitation – An extension of a specific course; a "review" session of sorts. Because some classes are so large, recitations offer a setting with fewer students where students can ask questions and get help from professors or TAs in a more personalized environment. As a result, it is common for most large lecture classes to be supplemented with recitations.

Rolling Admissions – A form of admissions. Most commonly found at public institutions, schools with this type of policy continue to accept students throughout the year until their class sizes are met. For example, some schools begin accepting students as early as December and will continue to do so until April or May.

Room and Board – This is typically the combined cost of a university-owned room and a meal plan.

Room Draw/Housing Lottery – A common way to pick on-campus room assignments for the following year. If a student decides to remain in university-owned housing, they are assigned a unique number that, along with seniority, is used to choose their new rooms for the next year.

Rush – The period in which students can meet the brothers and sisters of a particular chapter and find out if a given fraternity or sorority is right for them. Rushing a fraternity or a sorority is not a requirement at any school. The goal of rush is to give students who are serious about pledging a feel for what to expect.

Semester System – The most common type of academic calendar system at college campuses. This setup typically includes two semesters in a given school year. The "fall" semester starts around the end of August or early September and finishes right before winter vacation. The "spring" semester usually starts in mid-January and ends around late April or May.

Student Center/Rec Center/Student Union – A common area on campus that often contains study areas, recreation facilities, and eateries. This building is often a good place to meet up with fellow students and is most commonly used as a hangout. Depending on the school, the student center can have a huge role or a non-existent role in campus life.

Student ID – A university-issued photo ID that serves as a student's key to many different functions within an institution. Some schools require students to show these cards in order to get into dorms, libraries, cafeterias, and other facilities. In addition to storing meal plan information, in some cases, a student ID can actually work as a debit card and allow students to purchase things from bookstores or local shops.

Suite – A type of dorm room. Unlike other places that have communal bathrooms that are shared by the entire floor, a suite has a private bathroom. Suite-style dorm rooms can house anywhere from two to ten students.

TA (Teacher's Assistant) – An undergraduate or grad student who helps in some manner with a specific course. In some cases, a TA will teach a class, assist a professor, grade assignments, or conduct office hours.

Undergraduate – A student who is in the process of studying for their Bachelor (college) degree.

ABOUT THE AUTHOR:

I graduated from Lehigh in May 2003 and this is the first of what I hope to be many books I've written. I majored in journalism and was a member of Delta Phi fraternity. I was a writer and editor for Lehigh's official school newspaper, The Brown and White, for over two years and I had the honor and distinction of serving as editor in chief of the paper during my last semester at school. I also wrote two bi-monthly columns; "Senioritis," an opinion column about the trials and tribulations of being an outgoing senior; and "In Tune," a music column. All my work is archived and can be read on The Brown and White's web site, www.bw.lehigh.edu.

Please check out my blog, www.thisiswhatwedonow.com, as I update it daily and if you enjoyed my writing style in this book, you'll certainly want to read what I have to say every day. I'm co-creator and a contributing writer for www.worstofnewyork.com, a hilarious satirical web zine that's been steadily cultivating a rabid fan base. I was also a contributing writer for the 2005 Shecky's Bar, Club & Lounge Guide, so make sure to grab a copy of that as well. Feel free to e-mail me at larry.koestler@gmail.com – writers love e-mail, so don't hesitate to contact me. I thoroughly enjoyed writing this guidebook; and I look forward to more freelance work in the future.

I truly had an outstanding four years at Lehigh and wouldn't trade my college experience for anything. I had a great time writing this book and I hope it was informative as well as humorous. If you have any questions or comments, please feel free to e-mail me at LarryKoestler@collegeprowler.com. There are of a number of people who helped make this book what it is. I'd like to thank my parents, Scotty, ZW, Gold, Flax, Berbs, Lynch, Soul, Meat, Mush, my fraternity, Erica, everyone who responded to the surveys, everyone who buys this book, everyone who supports me now and in the future, and of course, the great folks over at College Prowler!

Larry Koestler

LarryKoestler@collegeprowler.com

Notes

Notes

Notes

Notes

Notes

Notes

Need More Help?

Do you have more questions about this school? Can't find a certain statistic? College Prowler is here to help. We are the best source of college information on the planet. We have a network of thousands of students who can get the latest information on any school to you ASAP. E-mail us at *info@collegeprowler.com* with your college-related questions. It's like having an older sibling show you the ropes!

Email Us Your College-Related Questions!

Check out **www.collegeprowler.com** for more details.
1.800.290.2682

Notes

Tell Us What Life Is Really Like At Your School!

Have you ever wanted to let people know what your school is really like? Now's your chance to help millions of high school students choose the right school.

Let your voice be heard and win cash and prizes!

Check out **www.collegeprowler.com** for more info!

Notes

Do You Have What It Takes To Get Admitted?

The College Prowler Road to College Counseling Program is here. An admissions officer will review your candidacy at the school of your choice and create a 12+ page personal admission plan. We rate your credentials with the same criteria used by school admissions committees. We assess your strengths and weaknesses and create a plan of action that makes a difference.

Check out **www.collegeprowler.com** or call 1.800.290.2682 for complete details.

Notes

Pros and Cons

Still can't figure out if this is the right school for you? You've already read through this in-depth guide; why not list the pros and cons? It will really help with narrowing down your decision and determining whether or not this school is right for you.

Pros	Cons

Notes

Need Help Paying For School?

Apply for our Scholarship!

College Prowler awards thousands of dollars a year to students who compose the best essays. E-mail *scholarship@collegeprowler.com* for more information, or call 1.800.290.2682.

Apply now at **www.collegeprowler.com**

Notes

Get Paid To Rep Your City!

Make money for college!

Earn cash by telling your friends about College Prowler!

Excellent Pay + Incentives + Bonuses

Compete with reps across the nation for cash bonuses

Gain marketing and communication skills

Build your resume and gain work experience for future career opportunities

Flexible work hours; make your own schedule

Opportunities for advancement

Contact *sales@collegeprowler.com*
Apply now at **www.collegeprowler.com**

Notes

Do You Own A Website?

Would you like to be an affiliate of one of the fastest-growing companies in the publishing industry? Our web affiliates generate a significant income based on customers whom they refer to our website. Start making some cash now! Contact *sales@collegeprowler.com* for more information or call 1.800.290.2682

Apply now at **www.collegeprowler.com**

Notes

Reach A Market Of Over 24 Million People.

Advertising with College Prowler will provide you with an environment in which your message will be read and respected. Place your message in a College Prowler guidebook, and let us start bringing long-lasting customers to you. We deliver high-quality ads in color or black-and-white throughout our guidebooks.

Contact Joey Rahimi
joey@collegeprowler.com
412.697.1391
1.800.290.2682

Check out **www.collegeprowler.com** for more info.

Notes

Write For Us!
Get Published! Voice Your Opinion.

Writing a College Prowler guidebook is both fun and rewarding; our open-ended format allows your own creativity free reign. Our writers have been featured in national newspapers and have seen their names in bookstores across the country. Now is your chance to break into the publishing industry with one of the country's fastest-growing publishers!

Apply now at **www.collegeprowler.com**

Contact *editor@collegeprowler.com* or
call 1.800.290.2682 for more details.

Notes